The Tigers in Your Dreams

Joyce

Enjoy every word

Sandra Butler Ladwig

This book was written to entertain everyone everywhere, including adoptive parents, siblings and everyone involved in the adoption triangle. It was written as though you and I were seated across from one another and I did most of the talking.

The Tigers in Your Dreams

Stories of adoptees reuniting with family members

Sandra Butler Ladwig

THE TIGERS IN YOUR DREAMS
Stories of adoptees reuniting with family members

This entire book was written and printed "without prejudice".

All names, dates and places in this book have been changed with the exception of the story about my Aunt Lavina and my own Mother's story.

Published by Sandra Butler Ladwig, Red Deer, Alberta

ISBN 978-1-77354-104-4

Publication assistance and digital printing in Canada by

PUBLISHING
PageMaster.ca

It is my pleasure to dedicate this book to all adoptive parents and everyone involved in the adoption triangle.

My Grandmother
always told me that
"the Tigers in your
dreams will never
catch you unless you
run away".

Table of Contents

INTRODUCTION

I have written this book for two purposes. The first is to provide information, assistance and support to adult adoptees searching for birth mothers, birth fathers and siblings. If an idea in one of the stories in this book provides an adoptee with new ideas, direction or renewed hope, then writing this book will have been my pleasure. The second purpose is to entertain everyone everywhere.

It would be difficult for anyone to write a "How To" book with step by step instructions on carrying out a search for a family member since there are seldom two searches alike. For that reason, I have tried to include a variety of stories that will provide a researcher ways and means to achieve his or her goal. All names, dates and places in this book have been changed with the exception of the story about my Aunt Lavina and my own Mother's story. The facts and emotions in this entire book are truthful as I personally experienced them, because I did not want any story to become fiction.

As a parent finder of 49 years, I have completed over 500 searches, and have guided in the neighbourhood of 1,000 adoptive parents, adult adoptees, birth parents and siblings who have carried out their own searches.

Although not always possible, I prefer that adult adoptees have their adoptive parents' consent and support prior to beginning a biological search. This respectful gesture not only opens the door to the two families becoming acquainted, it also provides adoptees with the love and support they may need if a reunion with a biological relative is denied. Following a reunion, I have asked adoptees how they feel toward their adoptive parents now that they have met their birth families, and many of them have said they love their adoptive parents twice as much as they did before – simply because of their parents' love, devotion and support. You will notice in this book I never use the inappropriate words "real mother," "real father" or "real parents."

Several people have asked me how and when I began searching for missing persons. My first job at the age of 18 was as a legal secretary in a law firm. I often found it challenging to locate a missing defendant so that he/she could be served with legal documents. My twin brother, who has similar "lost and found" senses, has been a private investigator most of his adult life.

When I hear the words "I have lost...," "Can you help me find...," or "Can you locate...." I go all out to achieve even the smallest find: a stolen leather jacket, a lost diamond ring, a lost wallet and yes – even a biological mother, a biological father, a brother and a sister.

For the first 26 years of our lives my brother and I

knew that we were adopted. The reason I say "knew" was because my twin brother told me that he had seen a document with "Certificate of Adoption" written across the top of it in large letters. It was grabbed out of his hands before he could read further. There were several other little clues as I was growing up. My brother wondered if we were even brother and sister, let alone twins.

At the age of 26, following an extremely frustrating attempt to find out information about my birth family, my Grandmother reluctantly told me that my twin brother and I were not adopted, however, our Mother was, but our Mother did not know it. I have included my Mother's story, "Love is Born in the Heart, Not Under it!" Although not as emotional as some of the other stories in this book, it is interesting and rewarding.

Some adoptees, who have had extreme difficulty finding information about their birth families, will relate to the devious lies and underhanded methods of searching they have had to undergo, especially from 1940 to 1985. Other than communicating with Family & Social Services, adoptees knew when they are trying to find out information by one means or another they must never divulge their reasons for wanting to find the person they are seeking. Telling the truth causes bureaucratic and sometimes household doors to slam shut hard and fast.

Some birth mothers who did not have the birth father's support nor their own family's support, had no choice but to go to a Home for Unwed Mothers. The result was that they were forced by their own families and by society into giving their babies up for adoption. Kahlil Gibran put it perfectly and precisely when he said:

The founding is an infant whose mother conceived him between love and faith, and gave birth to him between the fear and frenzy of death. She swaddled him with a living remnant of her heart and placed him at the orphanage gate and departed with her head bent under the heavy burden of her cross. And to complete her tragedy, you and I taunted her, "What a disgrace, what a disgrace!"

We don't do that any more.

Help arrived in the early part of the 21st Century by a man called "The Locator" who has a staff of about five. Also, the TLC TV show called "Long Lost Family" also opened the door for society to accept adoptees searching for their biological families as being a healthy and acceptable thing to do.

When I ask adoptees why they want to search for their birth mothers, the reply is always similar, "I want to know who she is, where she lives, and what she looks like. I want to know if I have any brothers and sisters. I want to know if anybody in her family looks like me!" Also, updated medical information is vital for several adoptees, their children and grandchildren.

Many adoptees feel that finding their biological families will finally create stability in their lives as well as closure. "CLOSURE" is the big word... I have observed this to be a true fact. Frightened and insecure adoptees have been totally transformed into stable, confident human beings with positive attitudes towards their past and their future after meeting their biological families. I have never met an adoptee who was searching for "a mother" or "a father" figure. They already have a mother and a father.

It is not only interesting, but fun to see adoptees compare elbows, knees, earlobes, gestures and personalities with members of their biological families. More important and gratifying are the warm and wonderful friendships that develop that will last the rest of their lives. Adoptees already have their own mothers and fathers, and therefore to meet that very special woman who gave birth to them is an added bonus in life. One adoptive mother said, "If I can love more than one child, then my children should be allowed to love more than one mother!" Most people who contacted me to do a search or assist in one – have been adoptive parents.

I should say here that there have been several occasions where adoptive parents do not want to assist their children in a search for their biological families and will not even talk about it. Some do not want to share the love they now receive from their children, some are just plain jealous and others are fearful that their children may find out that they were the result of a rape. In the two searches where this was true, the adoptee said, "I am surprised you went through with your pregnancy – I never would have – but I'm glad you did!" Remember too that when a baby was adopted, the birth mothers were 15 to 17 years old. Many adoptive parents tried to have a baby for at least a decade and were in their 30's when they chose to adopt.

Several birth mothers have said that if they had only known that their child survived, was happy and had good parents, they could have coped much better with their own lives. It was the "not knowing" that gnawed at them day by day, not to mention that big word, "GUILT!"

When adoptees experience a happy meeting with their birth mothers, their "reunion" can be electrifying. Many have said that, "it was like being on Cloud 9." The second and third meeting is comfortable. All meetings in the future are usually by phone, on special occasions and hopefully in person once or twice a year. Constant reinforcement is not necessary. Following a reunion, most adoptees have a confident and fulfilling future, and birth mothers shed the daily guilt they once felt in exchange for self-assurance in knowing that they had made the right decision.

A search for a birth mother can be extremely frustrating and difficult, especially for adoptees who have a common birth name, i.e. Smith, Jones, White, Anderson, Williams, etc. Also, research material is getting more and more difficult to obtain due to the Freedom of Information and Protection of Privacy Act. However, thunder and lightening struck when the all-important Ancestry DNA Kit came about. I know of one search that I worked on for 20 years, relying only on the information provided to adoptee Marion. After spending $7,000 on her search (that I could ill afford nor could she), I realized that all of the information provided to her by the Government was an out and out lie. A Licensed Search Agency could not find Marion's birth mother nor could I. The only way to find out who Marion's birth mother is, is to do a DNA Ancestry search.

Prior to the TV shows, I had always felt that it was vital for adoptees to contact their own birth mothers, birth fathers and siblings. It's not wrong for the TV show MCs to make contact, it's just my way of doing things.

When making contact, adoptees should keep in mind that the majority of birth mothers kept the birth and relinquishment of their children a secret from the rest of their families and the world, especially during the war years. It is totally unfair that an adoptee contact any member of the birth mother or birth father's families. Can you imagine an adoptee contacting an Aunt or Uncle who did not know about the birth and relinquishment? And of course – this was a good one: "Does February 14th 1955 mean anything to you?" Now, whosoever thought up that one surely did not put much thought to who was on the other end of the telephone.

It is my opinion that the manner in which a birth mother is contacted is crucial to the beginning and the successful development of a friendship between the adoptee and a birth parent. At the end of this book I have included my suggestion of "One Way to Contact a Birth Mother." Several birth mothers that I have met have said that they appreciated the manner in which they were contacted. I want to make it clear that I am also totally in favour of how the TV shows MC's contact a birth parent, a sibling or an adoptee. They are of course professional people, and I can assure you that I am not!

I have spent several years writing this book, only because I have been too busy assisting adoptees in order to complete it. I have also stopped repeatedly, trying to persuade the Alberta Government to allow adoptees, first mothers and first fathers to gain access to original birth registrations and the documentation contained in the adoption files and child welfare foster files. As a result, the Alberta Government established a "Reunion Registry" which meant that if an adoptee registers and a birth parent or sibling registers, they will be reunited by the Administrator of the Post Adoption Registry.

Following this step in the right direction, the Government then appointed a group of social workers in all cities in Alberta called "Government Licensed Search Agencies." These Licensed Search Agencies not only had access to the original adoption documentations on file, they also had full access to birth records, marriage records and death records. These search agencies not only had the pleasure of contacting a birth mother or birth father, they also charged their client a fee of up to $500.00.

I, for one, was very much against these agencies because of my belief that an adoptee should contact her/his own biological parent or sibling and of course should not have to pay such an exorbitant amount of money in order for the Agency to have that pleasure.

I did have one situation where an adoptee hired a Government Licensed Search Agency to access her adoption records and to contact her birth mother. The social worker, after receiving her fee of $500.00 found the birth mother and contacted her. She then phoned the adoptee and told her that her birth mother was not interested in a reunion with her. That was blunt! and was supposedly to be the end of her story..... Not so! When the adoptee contacted me – all upset and crying, I suggested that, with the little information she had, that we carry out a search for her birth mother ourselves. I did find her birth mother and taught the adoptee how to make contact in a very respectful manner. The adoptee phoned me back and told me that her birth mother had said, "I am so glad you contacted me yourself. I didn't like the attitude of the social worker who phoned me."

The very first adoption in Alberta took place in 1920. Prior to that time, families would simply go to a hospital, or an orphanage, choose a child, take that child home and change the name of the child to their own surname without having to legally do so.

Many years ago some babies were adopted with or without the consent of their birth mothers and seldom, if ever, with the consent of the birth father.

There are many stories involving the very sad experiences that birth mothers have had to endure, however, I am hopeful that each and every person involved in the adoption triangle has had some relief from the pain and suffering they once endured.

In 2004 I formed a Committee of four adoptees, two birth mothers, one birth father and one Aunt, and I appointed myself as the "Coordinator." We met with the Minister of Social Services and her Committee several times over a one year period. With the assistance of our MLAs, we were successful in opening the adoption records in Alberta on January 1, 2005. Hopefully access to adoption records will be legislated Canada-wide in the not-to-distant future!

I want to make it clear that I do not hold the social workers and nurses of today responsible for the things that went on in the old days.

I can tell you now that God has had something to

do with some of the searches I have been involved in. In those cases I was only used as a pawn.

In order that you, as a reader of my book, experience and feel the very different emotions in each true story, I would respectfully suggest that you read only one story per day.

Also, I should mention that when an adoptee plans to marry an adoptee, the two of them should compare notes. There was a situation south of Edmonton where a couple married and found out later that they were brother and sister.

....

To complete my introduction, I wish to state that I realize that I will never receive any recognition, a trophy or a medal, but I am happy to know that – in my lifetime I did something that will aid mankind by helping biological families and adoptive families meet one another and become friends. I have to say here that I had also been threatened for one reason or another, but still continued on. An adoptee, knowing that she/he was adopted is the truth – is it not? Whether or not to search for biological relatives is something that each person in the adoption triangle will decide to do or not to do themselves. Deciding not to search is just as acceptable as deciding to carry out a search. If anyone is suffering with their own personal decision, please remember what my Grandmother told me, "The Tigers in your dreams will never catch you unless you run away."

Sandra Butler Ladwig

CHAPTER ONE

WHAT IS IT LIKE TO HEAR A HAND

In 1976 I lived at Lougheed, Alberta. My Aunt Lavina lived in the same County, about 45 minutes south west in the little town of Forestburg. Her parents were Mr. & Mrs. Metias Hopfe of Hardisty. Aunt Lavina had one sister Hazel and two brothers.

Aunt Lavina telephoned me one morning. I was delighted to hear from her as she was the Aunt I had spent most of my summers with as a child. Not only did I recognize her Austrian accent, but she always greeted me with, "Hi there Old Girl!" I was very curious when she told me the reason for her call.

She asked, "Do you know a lady over there in Lougheed who looks like me?"

"Yes," I replied. "I do know somebody who looks a little like you."

She said, "So many people have told me that I have a twin over near Lougheed, and I am wondering if she could be my sister."

"Your sister!" I exclaimed. "You mean Hazel?"

"No!" Aunt Lavina replied. "Hazel is my foster sister and the Hopfe's are my foster parents. I have a sister I haven't seen since I was seven years old. She was only four years old when we were separated. Will you phone this lady who looks like me and find out if she could be my sister?"

"Sure! Of course I will," I replied.

I made a few telephone calls and found out that the lady she was referring to had not been adopted nor was she a foster child. I phoned Aunt Lavina back, giving her the message, but I had dozens of questions.

Aunt Lavina explained to me that she had been born "Profura Nikiforuk" in 1911 and was born at Hairy Hill, Alberta north of Edmonton. She had lived there with her parents and her brother and sister. She told me that her brother, "Aurel Nikiforuk" had been born in 1912 and her sister, "Marie Nikiforuk" in 1914. In 1918 a Social Worker named Charlie Hill (who many people will know), came to Hairy Hill and took Aunt Lavina and her sister Marie to an orphanage down by the Low Level Bridge in Edmonton. Aunt Lavina said that her brother stayed at Hairy Hill with neighbours.

"What happened to your parents," I asked.

Aunt Lavina said, "I was told that our mother died of Tuberculosis and our father went into a mental institution, but I don't know why."

"That was 58 years ago Aunt Lavina," I said. "You have never heard a word from your brother or your sister in all of these years?"

She replied, "I did try to find my brother back about 1948." A man came to our little town of Strome Alberta selling shoe laces. He was a deaf mute. As he stood at my doorway, we wrote notes back and forth. He wrote a note saying that there was a man by the name of Nikiforuk who was a deaf mute living at Youbou on Vancouver Island. When the man wrote that, I suddenly remembered that there was something different about my brother. He was blind, or deaf – something! In 1948 I wrote a letter to the Postmaster at Youbou asking if anybody knew of a family living in their area by the name of Nikiforuk. Unfortunately nobody replied to my letter."

"And what about your sister?" I asked. "Tell me about her?"

"My sister Marie was four years old and I was seven when we were taken to an orphanage in Edmonton down by the Low Level Bridge. Marie and I were always together, eating together, sleeping together, and playing together on the swings and teeter-totters out in the playground. One day when we were out in the playground, the Matron called Marie into the orphanage. I sat near the swings waiting for her to come back out to play. A long time later, the Matron came out and told me that Marie had gone home with a nice family who chose Marie to be their daughter.

Aunt Lavina said, "I cried for days and months because I missed my brother and sister so much." Then Aunt Lavina said, "One day a Mr. & Mrs. Hopfe came to the orphanage. They wanted a little girl seven years old to be a playmate to their daughter Hazel. They took me home with them to a town called Hardisty, and I grew up as "Lavina Hopfe."

When Aunt Laving grew up she married my mother's brother Gale and they had three children, Carmen, Delores and Genna. After Uncle Gale died, Aunt Lavina raised their three children on the income of a seam-stress.

I began the search for Aurel and Marie by sending for each of their birth certificates. The first certificate said "Marie Nikiforuk, born at Hairy Hill, Alberta on March 8, 1914," and the second said "Aurel Nikiforuk, born at Hairy Hill, Alberta on May 17, 1912." Parents on both certificates were listed as "Lazer and Domnica Nikiforuk." The question was, "Where are Marie and Aurel now and – what are their names now?"

I corresponded once again with Jan Richardson of Vital Statistics asking if they could search their marriage records to see if either Marie or Aurel had married in Alberta. Jan Richardson replied, saying that, "Unfortunately our records did not show a marriage for either of them between 1930 and 1950. There was also no Change of Names listed in our records for either of them."

I went through all of the Alberta and Saskatchewan telephone books, made a list of all Nikiforuk families and wrote to all of them asking if they knew an Aurel or a Marie Nikiforuk.

I then corresponded with Don Alexander of Family & Social Services in Edmonton asking if they had any records that would show where Aurel or Marie had gone to in 1918. He replied stating that many of their old foster files and adoption records had been destroyed. "Besides," he stated, "there were no adoptions in Alberta prior to 1920 and therefore we would not have had any records pertaining to the whereabouts of your Aunt's brother or sister."

I questioned Don Alexander once again, asking about the names of foster children and he replied that prior to 1920, a family simply took a child to raise and changed that child's name to their own surname without any legal requirement or documentation.

I phoned Aunt Lavina and told her about the Birth Certificates. She was pleased to know the Christian names of her parents. Then I told her about the marriage and change of name searches and what Mr. Alexander had told me.

I said to Aunt Lavina, "We now know that Marie's new family changed her name, but what about Aurel, who had supposedly stayed with a neighbour?" I asked, "Did you ever try to find out who he stayed with at Hairy Hill? Maybe the neighbour family he lived with would know where he is now?"

Aunt Lavina said that years ago she had contacted a Dennis Nikiforuk at Hairy Hill, who said that Aurel had lived with a Mahalcheon family for a few years and then he had gone to Edmonton and was living at the Salvation Army.

Aunt Lavina said that – in about 1960 she went to the Salvation Army in Edmonton, but nobody could remember her brother, Aurel.

I wrote a long letter to the Salvation Army in Edmonton asking if they had any record of an Aurel Nikiforuk living in one of their hostels back in the 1920's or 30's, and whether or not they might have a forwarding address for him in their records. A Major George Rikard replied to my letter, stating that it was very possible that Aurel had lived at the Salvation Army during that era, but unfortunately their old records had been destroyed.

When I phoned Aunt Lavina to tell her about this, she said she had been putting some thought to what Dennis Nikiforuk had told her and she remembered that possibly Aurel had lived at the Salvation Army for as long as ten years. We talked again about what she could remember from the age of seven. Again she said that she believed there was something different about Aurel. "He was deaf or blind – something...."

I sent a letter to the C.N.I.B. asking if they had a member named Aurel Nikiforuk who would now be about 64 years of age. I told them all about Aunt Lavina, Aurel and Marie. Then one of the Cookson families in Lougheed suggested that I also write to the Elks Purple Cross Deaf Detection Centre in Regina. A Brother Couling replied, stating that he was very interested in helping us find Aurel and would publish a monthly notice in their magazine, "The Canadian Elk." Brother Couling wrote back to me some time later, suggesting that I write a letter to the School for the Deaf in Winnipeg.

I wrote a letter to the School for the Deaf in Winnipeg. A few weeks later, they replied stating, "We have searched our files and cannot find any record of an Aurel Nikiforuk having attended our school between 1918 and 1940."

I then wrote to Joan Vanstone in Vancouver, the founder of a group known as "Parent Finders." I thought she may be able to help me even though I was not looking for a parent. Joan Vanstone wrote back to me saying that

Sandra Butler Ladwig

there was a "Harry Nikiforuk living at Lake Cowichan and she gave me his address.

At this point a great idea sprung into my head. I wondered if Aurel or Marie had ever written to their father at the mental institution? I wrote a letter to the Ponoka Mental Institute. They replied stating that Lazer Nikiforuk had been a patient there for about five years and then in 1924 he had been transferred to the Oliver Mental Hospital north of Edmonton. I decided to drive to Edmonton and go to the Oliver Mental Hospital.

The day I arrived I was a little excited and nervous. The waiting room was nicely decorated with red carpets and oak furniture. The lady I spoke with was very co-operative when I told her what I required. She left her desk for about 15 minutes, returning with a file folder in her hand.

"It was just as I suspected," she said. "Somebody cleaned out the contents of all of the old files years ago, maintaining only the file folders. Unfortunately there is absolutely nothing in Lazer Nikiforuk's file." I asked her why Lazer had been transferred from the Ponoka Hospital to the Alberta Hospital. She replied, "Likely there were no more funds available to keep him in Ponoka, and as a result, he was transferred into the care of the province."

I then went to the Land Titles Office and then to the Public Trustee's office, but found nothing except a Certificate of Title of property Lazer and Domnica had once owned at Hairy Hill. The property was taken by the province in lieu of taxes and Lazer's upkeep at Ponoka until the funds ran out.

I drove back to Lougheed. The next morning I

phoned Aunt Lavina to bring her up to date on what had transpired since our last conversation. Then Aunt Lavina said to me, "You know Old Girl, I have been thinking and thinking, racking my memory, and I seem to remember that when I was a very little girl, I played with a boy named 'Harry'." I couldn't believe my ears; "Harry Nikiforuk!" Joan Vanstone had told me about a Harry Nikiforuk living at Lake Cowichan, but I had not contacted him. I immediately phoned the long distance operator for British Columbia and obtained the phone number for Harry Nikiforuk in Lake Cowichan. I dialled Harry's number and let it ring about 20 times. I tried again an hour later, and then several times during the next two evenings. There was no answer. I then wrote a long letter to Harry Nikiforuk, telling him all about Aunt Lavina's search for her brother and sister. Three weeks later I still had no phone call or reply from him.

I should say here that – I always had two or three things on the go at once.

Since Aurel Nikiforuk would be turning 65 years old in about four months I thought he could possibly have already applied for his Old Age Pension.

He would have had to produce his Birth Certificate as proof of age. I phoned the Old Age Pension Office in Edmonton and asked for the addresses of Old Age Pension Offices for Alberta, British Columbia, Saskatchewan and Manitoba. Since we didn't have a photocopier in our small town, I had to type out all four letters. The next morning I went to our Post Office to buy some stamps and mail the letters. Since there were people lined up at the wicket, I unlocked my post office box first. I began thumbing through my mail. All of a sudden I noticed a letter from B. C. I tore it open. It was from Harry Nikiforuk. It began:

> I cried all day the day I received your letter. I have been searching for my two sisters Marie and Profura for 44 years. I am a deaf mute....

I didn't need to read any more. I immediately dashed out of the Post Office, jumped into my car and drove over to Forestburg.

I parked in front of Aunt Lavina's apartment, raced down the stairs and knocked on her door. Aunt Lavina opened the door. "Well hello there Old Girl!"

I walked into her little basement apartment for the first time. The same old antique dolls that were in her little two room house at Strome when I was a child, were propped up on a ledge in her living room, as well as numerous cupie dolls all dressed in crocheted dresses and picture hats. Then she sat down across from me. I couldn't wait any longer. I blurted out, "I have something for you." I reached in my purse and handed her the letter from Harry.

Aunt Lavina put on her glasses, chatting away as she opened the letter. I watched her eyes move down the page as she read, and then saw tears rolling down her cheeks.

"It's him," she said. "At long last. It's him." We sat side by side and together we read the remainder of Harry's letter.

> I am a deaf mute. I was born on May 17, 1912 at Hairy Hill, Alberta. My real name is Aurel Nikiforuk. My

wife's name is Dora, and we have four children – two boys and two girls. When I was 6 years old my two sisters left the farm and I was very sad. I stayed with a neighbour until 1926 when I went to the School for the Deaf in Winnipeg. I stayed there until I was 18 years old and then I moved to Edmonton.

I lived at the Salvation Army for ten years and searched everywhere for my two sisters. I couldn't get anybody to help me. Nobody could understand my sign language in order to realize how much I missed them.

About 1940 I hopped in a boxcar and headed for Vancouver and then came to Vancouver Island where I cooked in a logging camp until I was 60 years old.

My wife Dora is deaf also. This is why I cannot phone you. We are trying to get a special telephone where we can send messages on a keyboard.

I hope that I can meet my sister soon. I am so happy. I can hardly wait to put my arms around her after 44 long years of searching for her. Please write back.

Signed "Harry Nikiforuk. P.S. My daughter will be here on the weekend if you want to phone then.

We looked at the postmark and figured that the weekend he was referring to was probably last weekend. We were going to try to phone the following weekend.

I returned home still feeling the height of the day's excitement. I had read somewhere that the depth of your sorrow is the same dimension as the height of your happiness. I phoned Don Alexander at Social Services, as well as my family and gave them all the good news.

Sandra Butler Ladwig

The following weekend Aunt Lavina and I made a telephone call to Harry. A girl answered the telephone and seemed very excited when we told her who we were. She said she was Harry's daughter, and as we spoke to her we could hear her pause briefly after each statement and we somehow knew that she was telling her parents in sign language what we were saying. Aunt Lavina talked to her niece for a long time, telling her about all of the years she and Harry had been apart. I watched Aunt Lavina's gestures and listened to her speak, trying to catch up on a lifetime in just one telephone call. I then asked Harry's daughter if it would be possible for her parents to come to Alberta to meet Aunt Lavina. She said that her whole family were going to pay for plane tickets so that Harry and Dora could fly to Edmonton. She said she would let us know the arrival date, time and flight number. About a week later we received a phone call telling us that Harry and Dora would arrive on May 3rd at 10:00 a.m., Flight #212 from Victoria.

I tried my best to find Marie in the next four days. I phoned Don Alexander of Social Services once again, but he repeated that the old files dating back to 1918 had been destroyed by a summer student working in their office in 1965. I had a lump in my throat.

I decided to keep cheerful for Harry and Dora's arrival. I telephoned Major Rikard of the Salvation Army and brought him up to date on what had happened.

"I want to be there with you when they arrive," he said.

I gave him the date, time and flight number. A newspaper reporter from Edmonton phoned me that afternoon, asking if he could also be present at the arrival of Aunt Lavina's brother.

I was so excited the night before Harry and Dora were to arrive at the Edmonton International Airport, I could hardly sleep, but I was sure I was not the only one. Aunt Lavina, her daughter Genna, and Harry and Dora likely did not sleep either.

In the morning I drove to the Airport and waited for Aunt Lavina and Genna to arrive, which was only minutes later. We checked on the arrival of Flight 212 and it was going to be on time. We stood talking and then I noticed a man in a Salvation Army uniform. I approached him and asked if he was Major Rikard. "You must be Sandra," he said, as he shook my hand. I introduced him to Aunt Lavina and Genna.

I approached the Ticket Agent asking if there was anyone at the airport who knew sign language. The ticket agent said that one of their employees, Debbie McKeevers, knew sign language, and he promptly paged her. I waited with the Ticket Agent until Ms. McKeevers arrived. I explained the situation to her and she agreed to stay with us the entire time that her services would be required.

At 9:45 a.m. we all went over to the gate where Flight 212 would arrive. A man approached me and asked if we were waiting for Harry Nikiforuk. He introduced himself as a reporter from the *Edmonton Journal*. Enthusiastically he joined our little gathering.

At 10:00 a.m. a lady on the intercom announced "Air Canada Flight 212 from Victoria has now arrived." I had a lump in my throat and tears in my eyes. "Passengers arriving will come through Gate 12."

I stood back a few feet from everybody and watched. People started coming through the gate. Many of them had somebody meeting them, but it was not likely that any of them had a brother arriving that they had not seen in 59 years.

All of a sudden somebody shouted, "There he is!"

Aunt Lavina saw Harry. She raised her open arms and he ran directly to her. They both laughed and then they cried. Harry backed up slightly and stared fully at Aunt Lavina and through his tears he laughed with quiet excitement. I looked over at Major Rikard. There were tears running down his cheeks and his mouth was quivering. The reporter from the newspaper looked as though he was afraid to blink. Nobody spoke.

Uncle Harry turned around and took his wife Dora's hand and brought her toward Aunt Lavina. They hugged one another, both crying and trembling. Aunt Lavina started to introduce Harry and Dora to Genna, and at that point Debbie McKeevers stepped forward. She said something to Harry and Dora in sign language, and then she told Aunt Lavina, "You may speak to your brother and I will motion to them what you are saying."

Aunt Lavina wished to introduce everybody, first Genna and then myself. I introduced Major Rikard and the newspaper reporter to them. Harry was still laughing and crying. Dora was silently giggling. We moved away from the crowd, off to an area where we could all be alone together.

As the reporter, Major Rikard and I spoke, we all

watched the sign language between Debbie McKeevers, Uncle Harry and Aunt Dora. It was fascinating. At many times in my life I had noticed deaf people and their sign language, but because I had never personally known anyone who was deaf, I was a little afraid of infringing on their world. I knew in my heart that all of our lives would change now. We would all take the time to learn sign language.

After about one hour we bid farewell to Major Rikard and the reporter and thanked Debbie McKeevers for making the arrival of Harry and Dora so very special.

We left the airport, drove into Edmonton, met up with my twin brother George, and we all went to a restaurant for lunch. It was a joyous occasion. As quiet as it was between all of us, the excitement in all of our hearts was shouting "Hooray!" "Yipee!" "Halleluia!"

Dora began writing notes to us in her notebook, and we all took turns talking to her with a pen and paper. She signed to Harry what we were all writing back and forth. After dinner, my brother George said he had two surprises for us. He had been working behind the scenes. We all got into George's van and he drove us to an area on the north side of the Low Level Bridge, just north of the river. George parked his car beside a very large old brick building.

He turned around and announced, "This is the Orphanage that Aunt Lavina and Marie were brought to in 1918."

I couldn't believe my eyes. "How did you ever find it?" I asked.

"I phoned Mrs. Charlie Hill," he said, "and she gave

me directions. I checked old records at the library and confirmed that this is the very Orphanage that Charlie Hill had brought little children to back around 1918."

Aunt Lavina stared and stared at the building. I would imagine her mind wandering back to the days when she and Marie had played together on the swings and then that very sad day when they were separated perhaps forever. We all stepped out of the van and took pictures of everybody in front of the Orphanage.

When we were all back in the van my brother set off again. Nobody knew where we were going to next. We drove out toward Stony Plain Road. George pulled into a cemetery driveway. We all got out of the van and George directed us to a small gravestone that said "Lazer Nikiforuk."

Aunt Lavina said she had never known where her father was buried. She told me later that she assumed her mother was buried in an unmarked grave somewhere at Hairy Hill.

That evening Aunt Lavina, Genna, Harry, Dora and I headed for home. We followed one another until the Forestburg turnoff. We honked at one another as they turned and I continued on to Lougheed.

I began wondering about George having spoken to Mrs. Charlie Hill, the wife of the Social Worker who took Lavina and Marie from Hairy Hill to the Orphanage.

The next morning I telephoned Mrs. Charlie Hill and explained to her that we were searching for one of the children taken as a foster child from the Orphanage down by the Low Level Bridge. Mrs. Hill said, "I remember that a Mrs. Gutteridge ran that orphanage back in those early years. She is about 88 years old now. She may remember something."

Mrs. Hill gave me a phone number for Mrs. Gutteridge. I immediately telephoned her. When she answered, I introduced myself and then told her all about Aunt Lavina and Harry and their search for their sister Marie.

I told her all about Charlie Hill taking Marie and Profura to the Orphanage. I also mentioned that their brother Harry, had stayed on the farm for a time and then in 1926 he had gone to the School for the Deaf in Winnipeg.

She said to me, "I remember a young Harry Nikiforuk who stayed with us in our home for about a week back about that time. He was waiting for the weekly train that went to Winnipeg. He was a deaf mute and was going to attend the School for the Deaf in Winnipeg."

I was amazed that she could remember back 51 years ago. Anxiously I asked her, "Do you remember the names of the foster parents who took 4-year old Marie from the Orphanage in 1918?"

"I'm sorry, I don't remember," she replied. "We had many families coming to the Orphanage back then. However, we did keep a record of the names of those families on cards that were filed alphabetically in a long grey metal box."

"Do you remember what happened to that long grey metal box? Do you know where it might be now?" I asked anxiously.

"Wait now," she said as though trying to remember. After a long pause, she said, "When we closed down the Orphanage we gave that metal box to Social Services and

Child Welfare and as far as I know they must still have it."

I was so thankful to Mrs. Gutteridge for the information she had given to me. After I hung up I telephoned my brother George. He said he would go down to Social Services right away and talk to Don Alexander. I was on pins and needles the rest of that morning.

After lunch my telephone rang and it was Don Alexander. He said, "Your brother came down to our office this morning and told me what Mrs. Gutteridge had said. He and I went downstairs to the basement determined to find that long grey metal box. We looked through drawers and drawers of old filing cabinets in all of the rooms. We also went through shelves and shelves of old books, as well as old boxes. Everything down there is dusty and old and the lighting is very poor. We started at one end of a room and worked our way around it completely – before moving to the next room. Just when we were about to give up, we noticed a big cardboard box over in the corner of the last room. There were old dusty ledger books piled on top of one another. We took turns lifting each ledger binder out of the box and onto the floor. When George lifted the last binder out, we both stared in amazement and anticipation. There – on the very bottom – was a long grey metal box. We both grabbed for it at the same time, laughing at one another as we lifted it out and took it over to the light." Mr. Alexander continued:

"I pulled the drawer open and fingered through the alphabetical cards inside. There were two cards with the name "Nikiforuk" on them – one that said "Profura" and the other "Marie". On Marie's card were the words "Mr. & Mrs. Emil Norden, Mervin, Saskatchewan, 14 year foster agreement."

On the telephone that morning I think Don Alexander was as excited and ecstatic as I was. Nowhere else in this entire world was there any piece of information that linked Marie Nikiforuk to Mr. & Mrs. Emil Norden, other than what was contained on that little 3" x 5" card in that long grey metal box.

I told Mr. Alexander that I would phone him back within the hour. I dialled the area code for Saskatchewan; 1-306, and then information at 555-1212. I asked the operator for a listing for Emil Norden at Mervin Saskatchewan.

"I show one E. Norden," she said. She gave me that phone number. I thought that "E" must be "Emil."

I was shaking as I dialled Emil Norden's phone number at Mervin Saskatchewan. The phone rang exactly twice when a lady answered.

"Could I please speak with Mr. & Mrs. Emil Norden's daughter?" I asked.

"She replied, "I am their daughter Ellen. I am their only daughter."

Then I asked her, "Do you know where you were born?"

She replied, "I was born in a small town north of Edmonton in Alberta."

At that point I started to cry. Then I said, "Ellen, did you know that you have a brother and a sister?"

"Oh yes," she replied. "I did have a brother and sister,

but they both died of the flu when I was only four years old."

I laughed through my tears. "Oh no they didn't!" I replied. "Your sister is my Aunt and she lives at Forestburg Alberta. We have just found her brother – your brother – and he is at Forestburg visiting with her."

"Oh no!" she replied. "There must be some mistake. My parents told me that my brother and sister died when I was only four years old."

"Do you know that your name used to be Marie Nikiforuk?"

"No!" she replied. "I didn't know that. I am an orphan." Ellen seemed unconvinced that what I was telling her was true. I said to her, "You just stay right there. I'm going to have your sister phone you right away."

I knew that Ellen didn't believe me. How could she believe a total stranger rather than her own parents?

I phoned Aunt Lavina. Genna answered, and I could tell by her voice that she was inquisitive.

"Is Aunt Lavina there Genna?"

Yes?" she replied with a question in her tone.

"Could I speak with her please?" I said very calmly.

There was a short pause, and then Aunt Lavina said, "Well hello there Old Girl!"

I immediately began to cry, and through my tears I said, "Aunt Lavina, we have found your sister. She lives in Saskatchewan and I just talked to her on the phone a moment ago."

There wasn't a sound other than the whimpers of her tears. I knew that Harry and Dora would be watching Aunt Lavina's facial expression, wondering if she had just received good news or bad news. Genna took the phone from Aunt Lavina. I told Genna that Marie's name was now Ellen Norden and that she had been told by her foster parents that Lavina and Harry had died when she was only four years old. I gave Genna Ellen's phone number and then I hung up. I wish I could have been there in Forestburg to watch this wonderful occasion.

After I had hung up I phoned Don Alexander and my brother George in Edmonton and told them all about Ellen. I then looked upward and thanked God for guiding me and for giving all of us this beautiful gift.

Late that afternoon I phoned Aunt Lavina and asked her if she would like to go to Mervin, Saskatchewan the next morning. She was so excited to have spoken with her sister Marie that I think she would have preferred to leave right away – that very afternoon. We made arrangements for Aunt Lavina, Genna, Harry and Dora to pick me up at my house in Lougheed at 9:00 o'clock in the morning.

When I got off the telephone, my phone rang and it was a news reporter from CFRN Television, who had read an article in the Edmonton Journal about Aunt Lavina finding her brother. He wondered if he and his cameraman could come down to Forestburg to interview them. I said, "We have just found their sister Marie, and we are driving to Mervin Saskatchewan early in the morning to meet her. The reporter asked if he and his cameraman could come along with us. I agreed. We made arrangements to meet at the television station in Lloydminster.

The next morning we all met at the television station in Lloydminster. We all had lunch together and then set off for Mervin, turning left at North Battleford, going across a ferry to Turtleford, and then we turned south to our glorious destination. Mervin is a little town of about 150 people, one of whom was the answer to all of our prayers.

Our vehicle was the first to arrive outside of Ellen Norden's house. We stayed in the car until the television crew arrived. We all got out of our cars together. The reporter asked if we would all wait until his cameraman was set up ready to roll his film. I wondered if Marie was looking out of her window, curious about who we all were. Then the cameraman said, "Okay – ready to roll!"

Aunt Lavina walked up to Marie's door first, followed by Harry and Dora. I stayed back with the reporter watching this wonderful miracle that was about to happen. Standing next to me in spirit only, I felt the presence of Don Alexander and Janet Howell of Social Services, Jan Richardson of Vital Statistics, Rita of the Land Titles Office, Major George Rikard of the Salvation Army, Brother Lizette Couling of the Deaf Detection Centre in Regina, Joan Vanstone of Parent Finders in Vancouver, Mrs. Charlie Hill, Mrs. Gutteridge, and most important of all, my twin brother George.

Aunt Lavina knocked on the side door. Marie opened the door and came outside. Then Aunt Lavina threw her arms around her little sister Marie, and they both wept.

It was obvious that Marie was now convinced that this really was her sister Profura. They looked so much alike – they were like "the Bobbsy Twins." Then Harry stepped forward and hugged Marie, followed by Dora and Genna.

Harry was talking to Dora in sign language, wanting her to write some questions to Marie in her notebook. As I watched Harry, I noticed Ellen staring at the movements of his fingers. I remembered the little poem by Willard J. Madsen -

What is it like to comprehend
Some nimble fingers that paint the scene,
And make you smile and feel serene,
With the spoken word of the moving hand
That makes you part of the world at large.
What is it like to hear a hand?

NOTE: After Mr. & Mrs. Emil Norden died, Marie spent many months a year in hospital in a state of depression. Occasionally the doctors would send her home to Mervin for a change of scenery, only to find her back again two or three months later. She lived like that for many years, not having a relative in the world. Now that she has been found, Marie has tons of relatives. Marie moved to Forestburg and lived in the basement apartment across the hall from her sister Lavina. Then years later they shared a double room at the Galahad Health Care Centre.

Thank you to Mr. & Mrs. Emil Norden and thank you to Mr. & Mrs. Mettias Hopfe for raising these two little girls, who were then no longer two little orphans.

Mr. and Mrs. Emil Norden, Mervin Saskatchewan. 14 year foster agreement. Foster parents of Marie Nikiforuk.

Dora and Harry Nikiforuk's home in Lake Cowichan. When someone rings the doorbell the lights flash off and on.

Ellen Marie, Harry and Lavina together after 59 years apart.

At the airport

CFRN TV

Sandra and Genna Broder

Harry and sisters

Sandra and Ellen Marie

Sandra Butler Ladwig

Laverne and Ellen
Marie

Lavina Hodam
(Profura Nikiforuk)

Dora Nikiforuk, Harry Nikiforuk and
Sandra

CHAPTER TWO

BRING ME BACK A PAIR OF BLUE JEANS

The first half of this story, "my search for my brother Donald" – was written by Jill Peterson.

Times were very hard for my mother in England back in 1950. Our mother and father were separated. Mother could not afford the much-needed medicine I had to have. Since she was pregnant with a third child, nobody would hire her. Therefore, she had no other choice but to put my brother and me into a children's home where we would be cared for appropriately. My little brother Donald was 13 months old and I was only 2 years old when our Mother placed us in the Herne Bay Children's Home in Kent, England.

Mother came to visit us almost every week and promised that after her baby was born and she was able to find a job, she would come and take us back home again. Our father came to the Home to visit us once or twice in the early 1950's. Mother's visits continued until 1953, when she stopped coming altogether. We did not realize at the time that she had signed relinquishment papers, placing the two of us for adoption, on the condition that we be adopted together.

In October of 1953, when Donald and I were 5 and 6 years of age, a couple came to the Home to adopt a baby, but since there wasn't one available, they wanted to adopt me. There was no mention of them adopting Donald too.

At the time I left the Home, I didn't know what "adoption" meant, nor what leaving Donald would mean to my future. When I said "goodbye" to Donald, we kissed one another like we did every day. Both Donald and I had been told that I was going to Canada, but to a 5 year old, that meant that we were going shopping and that I would soon return to the Home and to my Donald. The last thing I remember was Donald yelling to me as I walked out to a car, "Jill, bring me back a pair of blue jeans!"

Shortly afterwards, my new mother, my father, their son Jeff, and I, flew in a large plane to Western Canada, severing all ties with my past. The pain of losing my brother haunted me for years afterwards. Almost every day something would happen that would remind me of him. I yearned to see him and I longed to be with him. Many nights I cried myself to sleep because I missed him so much. The one thing that I did have, which had been packed along with my few clothes in 1953, was a small photograph of Donald.

When I was 16 years old, I wanted to find Donald, but my adoptive mother and father discouraged me. They felt that they had furnished me with all of the love and affection I required, and had even given me a new brother – Jeff.

In my early 20's, I married, and in the next three years, we had two sons. That marriage did not work out. I divorced my husband and I then raised my sons alone until I was 28 years of age, when I again married. My second marriage was also unsuccessful, but I was determined to make it work, regardless of the physical beatings I experienced during my husband's almost daily drunken fits of rage. To my knowledge, Frank had never raised a hand to my children, but his mental abuse toward them was almost as bad. On the occasions I spent in hospital in Central Alberta, badly beaten, the children never once complained of being mistreated by Frank, and for that I was thankful.

When I was 34 years old, my adoptive parents, who now lived in Victoria, B.C. wrote to me and suggested I try to find my brother, Donald. I could not understand their change of heart, except that I remembered on one occasion when they came to visit, they must have noticed bruises across my forehead and down my cheek. Perhaps they felt I needed some kind of protection, or that I just needed someone who would love me as much as they did. I was pleased to receive their encouragement. Five minutes later I was on the telephone to England, and my search began.

My husband tried to discourage me every day, trying to make me feel that my brother wouldn't remember me, or that he wouldn't be interested in seeing me even if I did find him. He shouted "You are a nothing and a nobody! Who would want to know you!" I remembered the little picture of the adopted child, captioned "I know I'm Somebody – Cause God Don't Make No Junk!" I somehow knew in my heart that Donald would remember me and that he too longed for my touch.

It was 1982 that I began an all out search for Donald. My birth name was "Jill Theresa Peterson," born somewhere in Kent on July 17, 1948 and that my brother, "Donald James Peterson" was born about a year later. I did remember that Donald and I lived together for four years at the Herne Bay Children's Home. When I checked England phone books and telephone information in England, I found that the Home was no longer in existence. Strangely enough, I could not remember my birth mother or birth father's Christian names nor where they lived in England.

I wandered in and out of libraries for about 5 months, and made a few long distance telephone calls to England to no avail. I wrote dozens of letters to Peterson families in London, but nobody replied.

I then saw an ad in a local newspaper announcing

a "Birth Parent and Relative Group and Parent Finder's Group " that met once a month in our small city. I began attending the meetings and soon found that I was not alone. There were many people in the similar positions that I was in, all searching for a lost loved one. By listening to birth mothers speak, I realized how bad my first mother must have felt for the last 29 years, not knowing where Donald and I were. She would not have known that Donald and I were not adopted together as she had asked. Donald and I had not seen one another in 29 years either. "Donald, Donald Donald," I repeated softly to myself. Somehow repeating his name over and over again made me feel closer to him.

In 1983, I made a list of all of the Petersons living in Kent who had the initials "D" and DJ," and wrote dozens of letters that year.

In April of 1984 I wrote to a newspaper in Gravesend, Kent, asking for their assistance in finding Donald. I had a copy of Donald's photograph made and sent it along with my letter. Two months went by, when one morning I opened a letter from the Gravesend Examiner. Enclosed was an article entitled "Where Are You Donald?" and his photograph appeared at the top. I was thrilled and filled with hope. I ran to my mailbox every afternoon, but there was never anything there for me. Then about three weeks later, my telephone rang and an operator asked to speak with Jill Peterson. My heart pounded instantly. Then a man spoke,

"Is this my little Jill?" he asked.

"Yes!" I answered excitedly.

"This is your father speaking Jill," the man said in an

eager voice. At first – I thought it was some kind of joke, but after he told me all about himself these past 30 years, I believed it was my father on the other end of the phone. I was very pleased to hear from him. Then he said, "Just a minute – here's your mother."

After a short pause, a lady said, "Hello? Hello?"

"Yes, I'm here, mother. This is Jill." I started to cry when I heard her voice. My mother and I talked for over half an hour, England to Canada. Finally, I asked her if she knew where Donald was. She explained to me that she did go to visit us in 1957 and was very upset to find that I had been adopted, but Donald was still there. She said she was furious that we had not been kept together. Then, switching the conversation to her, she told me that she had remarried and had five more children, plus the one little girl who was a full sister to me. I changed the subject back to Donald, questioning my mother and father about his whereabouts, but they both said that neither of them had seen him since 1957. They assured me that, although they had built separate lives from one another, I would always be welcome in either of their homes and as a part of their families. After we hung up, I felt very strangely alone. There was only one family I truly belonged to and that was the family of Donald James Peterson – wherever he may be. He was my family!

In August of 1984 I wrote a letter to the British Agencies for Adoption & Fostering. They sent me a pamphlet entitled "If you are Adopted." They advised me that in order to find my brother, I would have to hire a professional researcher, which they said would be very expensive. If I could afford 30 pounds plus a fee, they suggested that I write to St. Catherine's House to see if they could suggest someone who would do a search for Donald's birth and marriage certificates. I wrote a letter back to British Agencies for Adoption asking if Donald had been adopted. They advised me that before they could release any information to me I would have to come to England, make an appointment to see a Councillor and if he felt I had a legal right to information about Donald, he would release information to me. They wrote, "No information could be released by mail." I decided to write to St. Catherine's House for my own birth certificate and I sent them 10 pounds.

In the meantime, I wrote a letter to the General Register Office in Hants and they advised me that, "they were precluded, under the Adoption Act, from providing any person with information which would link the birth entry of an adopted person." They said that what they could do was enter my name and address in their Registry so that if Donald ever approached them wanting information about me, they would be at liberty to release it to him. I filled out the form provided and forwarded it back to them.

I was feeling that my search for Donald might be hopeless, and as my husband Frank had said belligerently many times, perhaps if I did find Donald he wouldn't remember me or he may not want to be found by me. I remembered Donald's last words as he shouted, "Bring me back a pair of blue jeans." At that time he was likely about a size 6. That phrase gave me hope, regardless of what my husband said. I knew that my brother would want to see me. I phoned my adopted mother, and hearing how sad I was, my mother said:

> I should have told you this years ago. When you were only 16 years old, your father and I received a letter from a Social Worker in England, stating that Donald Peterson had been in touch with her, and that Donald wished to correspond with his sister, Jill Peterson. We were afraid to tell you about Donald back then, for fear that you would go flying back to England to be with him, and we would never see you again. Please forgive us.

I was shocked, but also enlightened. I asked my mother, "Do you still have the letter?"

"No dear. I think it was lost in one of our moves, but I seem to recall though, that the Social Worker's name was Mrs. Joyal, or Royal."

After I hung up the phone that day, I first felt cheated by my own parents, but then, as I thought about it, they were probably right. I would probably have flown back to England to be with Donald.

In October of 1984 I finally received my own Birth Certificate. There were words written in the last column in somebody's handwriting, which read "Adopted November 3, 1953." I was thrilled to see those words. If I could get Donald's Birth Certificate, there could be a notation that he was also adopted.

In the early winter of 1984 I again wrote to British Adoption & Fostering, asking if they knew of anybody who could do a search for a birth registration and possibly a marriage record at St. Catherine's House. A Mrs. Stafford replied that, "although it is not our general practise, I went down to St. Catherine's House and found a birth registration for a Donald James Peterson in the third quarter of 1949, Ref. 9d45." She had also noticed a marriage for a Donald Peterson in the second quarter of 1968, a Donald J. Peterson in the third quarter of 1969, and a Donald J. Peterson in the first quarter of 1971. Mrs. Stafford also explained that there was no way of knowing whether any of these entries could be my brother. The only way to find out for sure would be to send her 30 pounds and she would request all three marriage certificates. Unfortunately, I didn't have 30 pounds, but I immediately forwarded 10 pounds to Mrs. Stafford asking if she could please again visit St. Catherine's House and obtain the birth registration for Donald James Peterson in the third quarter of 1949, Ref. 9d45. I waited six weeks until the letter finally arrived from Mrs. Stafford. I unfolded Donald's birth registration, and quickly glanced at the right hand column. I sighed with relief to see that it was blank. There was no notation of an adoption having taken place. Donald was born on August 3, 1949.

Mrs. Stafford's letter contained valuable information. She said that I should write to the Kent County Council and ask if they have the records from the Herne Bay Children's Home. I immediately wrote to them. On May 14, 1985, I received a reply from the Kent County Council stating that the records from the Home were in their care, and they had positively found Donald's records. The letter continued:

We have had no information about Donald since August

of 1967 when he became 18 years of age. At the time he was in the Herne Bay Home, it is stated that he was somewhat unsettled and caused some anxiety about his behaviour, but it says a lot for him that he completed the course, and I daresay some of his behaviour was normal for a teenager with an unsettled background. Our records indicate that when he left school it was his intention to take a hairdressing course at the Erith Technical College. The last known address we have for him is in care of a Mrs. Holmes, 156 Farnham Road, Sidcup, Kent. I do not know if he kept in touch with the Holmes family or not. I took the liberty of telephoning the Erith Technical College, and from their records, they advised that when Donald left the College, he opened a hairdressing business in the Bexleyheath area of London, but a few years later, sold his business and went racing but – what kind of racing they did not know.

I was ecstatic! I now had information about Donald up to and even beyond 1967. My first quest was to try to find Mrs. Holmes of 156 Farnham Road, Sidcup. I phoned information in England, but there was no listing for a Holmes in Sidcup at all. I then wrote to 156 Farnham Road asking the owner of the house if he would know the whereabouts of Mrs. Holmes. I never did receive a reply to that letter.

I tried every means I could think of to find Donald that winter, to no avail. One evening I went to a Birth Parent & Relative and Parent Finders Group meeting, mostly to receive some encouragement to keep on searching. I met a lady there who had searched for missing persons for many years. She gave me the support I needed.

Only two days later, my husband came home late

one evening. He had been drinking. He grabbed me and threw me across the room. He was yelling something about me not searching for Donald any more. I couldn't understand his incoherent phrases, "He's not welcome in my house!" "He hates you!" "He doesn't want you." "Nobody wants you!" That was the night of the most horrible beating I had ever experienced. When Frank passed out, I grabbed some clothes for the children and me, my whole file on my search for Donald, and we left – making our new home a Women's Shelter in a nearby City. It was there that we lived for several weeks. My search for Donald was over.

Much to my surprise, one evening the lady I had met at the group meetings came to the Women's Shelter to talk to me. She offered to carry on my search for Donald. I was so happy that somebody was willing to help me.

A PAIR OF BLUE JEANS – WHAT SIZE

The second half of this wonderful search for the love of a long lost brother, was written by me – Sandra Ladwig.

(Author's note: I have included all of the intricate details of this search in England for the benefit and purpose of providing insight to adoptees who may be searching for a family member in Great Britain. Although records are open to the general public for viewing, someone must be hired to do the searching, which can be very costly.)

The night I met Jill at the Women's Shelter, I was shocked at the sight of her facial bruises. I imagined that the pain she felt emotionally was likely more excruciating than what I could see. Jill was very petite and extremely beautiful, with long white-blonde hair to her waist, much like the girl in the Avon ad. On all other occasions I had met Jill, her voice was soft and melodic, but this night she sounded like a wounded animal with no will to live.

When I left Jill that night, carrying with me the file on her search for Donald, I was thankful that she had two sons to live for; otherwise she may have chosen Heaven over the daily hell she had been enduring since her marriage to Frank. I also left her with an extremely valuable feeling of "HOPE" for the future.

I dove right into Jill's search. I began by going through the London Telephone Book, making a note of various hairdressing shops in what I thought was the Bexleyheath area of London. I wrote to each one. I then wrote to hairdressing supply companies and hairdressing insurance companies to see if anyone may have known a Donald Peterson.

Since I was not sure what type of racing Donald had taken up, I wrote to dog racing, car racing and horse racing clubs. I felt sure that one of my letters would eventually reach somebody who knew Donald.

On April 1st, I wrote a letter to a lady I knew in Kent – a Doreen Alan. I told Doreen all about Jill's search for her brother, and asked her for information and her opinion on various channels I could pursue. On May 23rd, Doreen answered all of my questions:

1. It would not be possible for me to do a motor vehicle operator's license search for Donald in Swansea,

Wales, as those records are confidential and can only be released to a member of Scotland Yard.

2. I contacted the Salvation Army, who agreed to assist in trying to find Donald. I gave them all of the particulars you told me about him. (This was encouraging because the Salvation Army in England have about a 70% success rate in locating missing persons.)

3. I am enclosing the names of newspapers in the Bexleyheath area of London, and those near the Erith Technical College and near the Herne Bay Children's Home. One or all of them may agree to publish an article about Jill searching for her brother Donald.

4. I tried every avenue to find Mrs. Joyal or Mrs. Loyal, who had written to Jill's adoptive parents when Jill was 16 years old, to no avail.

5. I tried to find Mrs. Holmes who had lived in Sidcup, Kent, to no avail.

6. I made numerous phone calls to racing clubs, to no avail.

Doreen saved me months and months of searching by means of mail and telephone calls.

On May 28th I wrote a letter to New Scotland Yard, requesting their assistance. I gave them every piece of information I had on Donald James Peterson, and advised them of all that had been done so far in an effort to find him. On July 4th Commander B14 replied to my letter.

"Searches have been made in our records and those

of the Drivers' Licensing Centre at Swansea, Wales, unfortunately without success. Local police have made enquiries at all of the Bexleyheath hairdressing salons, but everyone spoken to had not heard of Mr. Peterson. Police also visited two D. J. Petersons living in the Bexleyheath area whose addresses had previously been given in the northwest Kent area, unfortunately to no avail. The Press Liaison Officer passed on the information to the local paper, the "Bexleyheath & Wellington Observer," and an article appeared in the paper on 10 June, but again there was no response. I regret that – despite extensive inquiries, the Metropolitan Police are unable to assist further."

I was very sad, but not altogether dismayed. I then wrote a letter to the Kent County Constabulary Police Station at Gravesend in Kent. They replied on September 5th stating that they had exhausted all avenues of inquiry but were unsuccessful in tracing Donald.

In October I wrote to Immigration Canada in Ottawa Canada, and their reply advised me that Donald James Peterson had never entered Canada during the period January 1, 1952 to November 14, 1985.

Letters from hairdressing salons and racing clubs began arriving, but the replies all stated that nobody could remember Donald.

I wrote to the British Consulate General in England requesting addresses for the Passport Office, the Department of Health & Social Security, and the Board of Inland Revenue. The Consulate General assured me that if Donald was in Great Britain, he would have to have compulsory health insurance coverage and he would have to pay income tax to the Board of Inland Revenue.

It seemed to me that if Donald was not in Great Britain, he may have gone on to a racing circuit perhaps through France and Morocco, and possibly may have stayed there, which would account for the fact that he was not in Great Britain.

I wrote a letter to the Passport Office in England asking if Donald had ever applied for a Passport. I then asked if it would be possible for someone to be situated outside of Great Britain and apply back to Great Britain for a Passport. Their reply arrived about two months later, stating that Donald had in fact applied for a Passport when he was 12 years old, but was denied, and that he had not since applied. They stated that all British subjects must apply for a Passport from Great Britain and not outside of Great Britain.

I concluded that – just because Donald didn't have a driver's license didn't mean he wasn't in Great Britain. Perhaps he didn't own a car.

I then wrote a letter to the Department of Health & Social Security and to the Board of Inland Revenue. Two months later, I received replies from both the Department of Health and Inland Revenue, neither having any record of a Donald James Peterson born August 3, 1949.

It was discouraging to find that Donald was not in Great Britain, and yet he had never left Great Britain. How could that be? I wasn't sure what to do next. I remembered a small saying by Robert Brault that gave me a little bit of a shove:

*"Where the Loser sees barriers,
the Winner sees hurdles!"*

and what Thomas Edison said:

*"The most certain way to succeed is
always to try just one more time."*

I knew all about hurdles. I wouldn't even dream that Donald could be deceased. My only other thought was that perhaps Donald had changed his name. I read every word on Donald's birth certificate, but there was absolutely no reference to a name change or to another birth certificate.

I wrote a letter to St. Catherine's House and asked if it would be possible to order a marriage certificate for a Donald Peterson, married in the first quarter of 1968, another married in the 3rd quarter of 1969 and a third married in the first quarter of 1971 without knowing the Reference numbers allocated in their records. They replied that they could send me the certificates upon receiving 10 pounds for each request. They did, however, provide me with the names of the brides and the locations where the three marriages took place. I was unable to find two locations on a map of England, but the third was located in the Sandwell District. I wrote a letter addressed to: "The Registrar, Sandwell District, 50 miles West of London England." Two months later, and much to my amazement, I received a reply from the Registrar that said: "Your letter, after travelling a fair circuit of England, arrived at my office. I regret to inform you that the Donald J. Peterson who married in Sandwell was not born on August 3, 1949."

I put off ordering the other two marriage certificates for the time being, mostly because I didn't have $50.00 to spare. Jill went back to her husband just before Christmas. He promised her that if she would come back to him, he would never hurt her again.

I met Jill for lunch one day in early January and brought her up to date on all of the letters and replies that had been sent and received. She seemed generally sad. The restaurant we were in was rather warm. When Jill took off her jacket, I noticed bruises all down her forearms, and dark grey stripes at the back of her neck. Jill noticed me looking at the bruises on her arms. I asked, "Have you ever thought of getting a Restraining Order?"

"There would be no sense," she replied. "He wouldn't stay away from me! He would find me no matter where I went."

I suggested that she move far away, but she said, that Frank would only come after her, beat her up again and bring her back. When I left her that day, I was very worried about what was to become of her. Her situation made me move forward more than fiercely to find her brother because I felt very much alone in this quest. I just knew in my heart that Donald would step in and protect her.

The next day I wrote a letter to the Kent County Council who had the records of the Herne Bay Children's Home in their office. I explained to them that Health and Tax records proved that Donald was not in Great Britain, and yet he had never left Great Britain. I asked the question: "Is it possible that Donald may have changed his name?" A month later I received a reply from them, stating,

"There is a small notation on one form in Donald's file where the word "Michael" is written in someone's handwriting and in brackets. The context of information around that name refers to Donald. It's possible that he changed his name to Michael, or just preferred to be called "Michael."

I was so excited that I immediately wrote letters back to New Scotland Yard Commander B14, the Department of Health & Social Security, and the Board of Inland Revenue, asking each of them if they would re-search their records for Donald under the name of "Michael Peterson, born August 3, 1949, and if his address was found, would they forward the enclosed letter on to him.

I enclosed a lovely letter as though written by Jill, telling Donald all about "my" search for him and "my" hope that someday "I" would find him so that I could collect all of the kisses he owed me, and of course to give him that pair of blue jeans he had once asked for.

On August 1st I received a short letter from the Department of Health & Welfare in Newcastle. The stationary was only 3" x 5." It stated:

The letter you sent me for forwarding to Michael James Peterson, born August 3, 1949, has been passed to the last known address of a person who may be the person you asked about.

That's all the note said, but I was grateful for those

few words. There was now finally a new glimmer of hope.

On the morning of August 28th I was at work as usual. My daughter telephoned me at 11:00 a.m. Knowing the magnitude and importance of Jill's search for Donald, she said, "Mom, there's a letter here from Michael J. Peterson in Ireland." I immediately started to cry and couldn't answer her. My boss came out of his office, and seeing that I was crying, he put his arm around my shoulder, trying to console my tears. I could not stop sobbing long enough to tell him about Donald. Finally I blurted out the words, "These are happy tears!" Then I had an all-out good cry. Ten minutes later, I went into my boss's office and briefly told him all about Jill's search for Donald, and the letter that had just arrived at my home.

"Go and get it!" my boss said, sharing in my excitement.

On the 2 mile drive home, a great feeling of contentment came over me. I crossed the bridge that connects the south and north of our City and stopped at the red traffic lights. All of a sudden a great realization came over me. (And "yes" you may begin to cry with me.) I raised my eyes to the blue sky above, and with a peaceful smile, I said right out loud, "You did this!" I realized at that moment that I had only been used as a tool, someone through whom a beautiful miracle was about to take place.

I drove up the hill, turned onto my street, drove into the driveway, put the car in park, excitedly ran into the house, grabbed the letter, kissed the letter, kissed my daughter, ran back to the car, and drove back to work.

I dashed into my boss's office, and sitting there together, both of us filled with anticipation, I opened the blue onionskin airmail letter. It read:

"Dear Jill:

"I was astonished and overjoyed to receive your letter forwarded to me by the Health Office in Newcastle. I must have read it 100 times tonight already, not believing that it really could be from you. There's so much to say, but I don't know where to start. So much has happened over the years, some of which I only want to forget.

"You have no idea what it means to me to know that you and I could soon be close again, how it should be. Oh! Jill, I've missed you. As you can see from the above address, I now live in Ireland and have done so for some 17 years. I am married and have a son Richard, who is ten. I teach hairdressing at our local college of further education.

"You said very little in your letter about your personal life. Are you married? Have you any children? There's so much to talk about, that it is impossible to put it all down in one letter. You should have seen me when I received your letter. I was like a little boy again, reaching immediately for the Atlas to locate your home. My wife Maria is in the travel business and is checking cheap ways to get to Canada.

"I have tried to visualize how you look and enclose some rather bad photos of us on holidays last year, but at least it will give you some idea. I could go on for hours, but am desperate to get this in the post in the hope that you will phone me. I did try to get your phone number, only to be told that you were not listed. One thing I have not told you, and that is – I no longer call myself Donald, but changed my name to Michael. I just did not like my name. I think that when you see me you would agree that Mike suits me better. Never fear, I will never want to forget my cheeky little sister. I hope that when you receive this letter you waste no time in contacting us. All my love, Michael, XXO. P.S. I love you!"

(Just to be on the safe side, I photocopied Michael's letter, photographs and the envelope containing his return address. You never know what Jill's husband might do if he finds this letter on Jill.)

In the photograph enclosed, Michael is wearing shorts. His hair is dark and curly and he has a moustache. He is very handsome and well tanned. Maria has dark short hair – she is very pretty and has a slim figure. Richard looks just a little older than the photograph Jill has of Donald when he was 5 years old.

In mid-afternoon I telephoned Jill and asked her to meet me at 7:00 p.m. in a restaurant not far from her house. I waited and waited in the restaurant, but she did not arrive. I phoned her again, and was surprised when she answered.

I said, "Are you coming to meet me Jill?"

She replied "It's impossible for me to get away tonight. Frank is home and he's drunk."

I realized I had to tell Jill the truth. I said slowly and precisely: "I have found Donald! Please come and meet me."

There was a gasp on the telephone and then she said, "I don't care what I have to go through. I will be there as soon as I can get there."

About an hour later, Jill came dashing in the door of the restaurant seemingly out of breath.

When she sat down, we both went through all of the letters and replies since our last visit together. Then she paused before turning over to the last page. She took a deep breath, turned the page, only to see that it was blank. I reached in my purse and handed her Donald's letter. I could see that she was shaking as she opened it. She sat quietly, reading every word slowly. Tears started rolling down her cheeks, and I thought to myself, "let them flow like rivers and lakes." I ordered a pizza and wine, and while we ate and drank, Jill must have opened and closed Donald's letter at least a dozen times. We wondered what time it was in England right then, figuring that when it was nightfall here, it must be dawn in England.

Jill smiled and laughed, enjoying the peaceful anticipation of tomorrow. Then Jill looked at me with a serious look on her face. She started to say something and then stopped. Tears started rolling down her cheeks. Then after a long pause, she swallowed, looked at me again, and then said, "I was going to end my life tonight after Frank passed out. I had it all planned."

I don't know what I felt at that moment, whether it was horror, or fear, or gratitude, but I did remember back to that morning when I looked upward to the Heavens, and now I wondered, "Why did this letter arrive this very morning – why not tomorrow morning?" and I knew, as we have always known, that there is a God up there looking after each and every one of us.

> (Author's Note: When I left Jill that night she was dancing around in the parking lot, chanting "I have a brother, I have a brother. Donald, Donald Donald!, Then she laughed and said, "Michael, Michael Michael."

Jill telephoned Donald when she arrived home that very evening, and she told me that they talked for two hours. I wrote letters to everybody in England who had helped find Donald – thanking them all for their assistance and telling them all about the outcome.

Within that month, Jill obtained a Restraining Order from the Courts, and it was served upon her husband by two Police Officers who stood in her kitchen while Jill packed.

Jill and her two sons moved far away where nobody would ever find them, with the exception of her adoptive parents, and of course Michael. A few months later, Jill phoned me to say that her brother, now Michael, his wife Marie and their son Richard had visited with her for two weeks and that she was planning a trip to Ireland in the spring. I asked her one question: "Did you ever buy Donald that pair of blue jeans?"

She replied, "Yes. Just as a joke, I bought him a boy's size 6."

Sandra Butler Ladwig

CHAPTER THREE

A STICK OF GUM
FOR JOEY

Patsy lived in a small town south of Calgary where she managed a Royal Canadian Legion. Patsy had unsuccessfully tried to find her brother Joey for many years. She had even hired private investigators, but they too were unsuccessful in finding Joey.

Patsy was born in a small town close to a major city in Saskatchewan. Her birth mother Anna and birth father Jacque were married to one another, but since Jacque lived a life similar to that of Al Capone, Anna feared for the safety of their daughter Patsy. Anna found a farm family who agreed to legally adopt Patsy when she was only two years old. Jacque agreed to sign the relinquishment documents for the sum of $100.00. At the time of Patsy's adoption, Anna was seven months pregnant with Joey. After Joey was born, Patsy often played with Joey when Anna came to visit her. Both children were sad every time Joey had to leave.

One day when Anna and Joey came to visit Patsy, Anna asked Patsy's adopted parents if they would consider raising Joey as well. At that time Patsy was five years old and Joey was three. Anna whispered that she was afraid of what might happen to Joey if he remained with her and Jacque any longer. She wanted Joey to be somewhere safe, and preferred that he be with his sister Patsy. After talking it over, Patsy's adoptive parents agreed to adopt Joey.

When Patsy's adoptive parents went to see a Social Worker in a large gymnasium in Saskatchewan, both Patsy and Joey sat next to one another waiting for the decision that would allow them to be together forever. Patsy's adoptive parents were ushered into another room to speak with the social worker.

"Am I going to come and live with you Patsy?" Joey asked hopefully.

"I sure hope so," she replied. "We're going to try to adopt you so that you can come and live with us. That's why we're here," Patsy said.

Patsy and Joey sat side by side holding hands for over an hour. Joey seemed frightened, but Patsy continuously reassured him that everything would be okay. Without saying it in so many words, Patsy expected that Joey would go home with them that very day. When Patsy's adoptive parents and the social worker came back to the gymnasium, the social worker held out her hand motioning for Joey to take her hand.

Joey started to cry and ran to Patsy. She took his hand and then she hugged him. She reached into her pocket and took out a stick of gum and handed it to Joey, hoping he would enjoy her little gift.

The social worker took Joey's hand and led him away, but the whole while, Joey was facing backwards reaching out to Patsy, yelling her name over and over again. Then he was out of sight.

Patsy's adoptive parents explained to her that they had made application to adopt Joey, but the social worker told them that they would not hear her final decision for at least two weeks.

At the end of two weeks, the adoptive parents telephoned the social worker. She said, rather bluntly, "I am sorry. Joey has been placed with another family."

Patsy's adoptive father pleaded with the social worker, but she simply repeated her decision, "Joey has been placed with another family – it is for the best!" She would not give any reason for her decision. When Patsy was told, she cried and cried.

While Patsy was growing up she always wanted to try to find Joey, but her parents told her that it was impossible. They had no idea who had adopted Joey.

When Patsy was about 18 years old, she recalled talking to a man who told her that her birth father Jacque had recently died. Patsy asked many questions about her father. She gathered from the information told to her that her father had been a type of mafia leader. Patsy asked a lot of questions in the small town where she lived, but everybody had been afraid to say anything about Jacque for fear of what he might do to them, even from the grave. One man that Patsy spoke to told her that he knew nothing of Patsy's mother Anna, other than the fact that she had been very ill many years ago and had left her husband.

Although Patsy married in her early 20's, she said that she still felt lonely without knowing where Joey was, and especially after her adoptive parents died. Her exact words were, "Families always get together – parents, grandparents, brothers and sisters, cousins, aunts and uncles, but I have no family of my own. My husband comes from a large family but I have nobody except my brother Joey – wherever he is. I have no idea who adopted him."

Patsy asked if I would help her find her brother Joey. We wrote a letter to the Government asking for the status of Joey's care up to the age of 18 years. We were sure that the Government would not give Patsy her brother's adoptive name. When the reply arrived, it stated:

> Joey went into a foster home and remained there until his 18th birthday. His name was legally changed to the name of his foster parents when he was 10 years old. From the reports made on Joey's development throughout the years, he had a normal childhood, attended junior high and high school, graduating from Grade 12. It was his intention at that time to go into Engineering when he left school.

In a second letter, we inquired as to the policy of foster children in that province, and if any of their siblings could know the identity given to any brothers and sisters especially after reaching the age of 18 years. Their reply stated that "Siblings have a right to know the identity and last known whereabouts of a brother or sister provided that the brother or sister had never been adopted."

Patsy and I were ecstatic to read that letter because it stated ..."that siblings have a right to know the identity and last known whereabouts of a brother or sister provided that the brother or sister had never been adopted."

We wrote back to James Gordon, the Director of Social Services, requesting information as to Joey's new name and his last known whereabouts. When the reply arrived, I was upset but Patsy was furious. It seemed as though Mr. Gordon made up rules as he went along. The letter read:

> It is true that we do supply identifiable information to a sibling of a foster child, however, since Patsy and Joey had never lived together under the same roof, we are unable to provide you with any further information.

This was definitely slamming the door to any future requests.

I telephoned Mr. Gordon asking why the discrepancy. He said that the social workers in his department had a meeting, and that it was their decision that they could not release any information in this particular case. He ended his letter saying that there was nothing he could do.

I advised Mr. Gordon that if he did not give Patsy her brother's name and last known whereabouts, we would put a story into his local newspaper asking for the public's assistance in locating Joey.

His very lame reply was, "I guess you'll have to do what you have to do!"

Naturally, I didn't think Mr. Gordon took me seriously – perhaps he thought I was only bluffing. For sure, Mr. Gordon did not know me. I was determined to break their "convenient non-policy" decision.

I wondered if the social workers were trying to hide something, and were afraid of the truth eventually coming out as to why Patsy's adoptive parents were not allowed to adopt Joey. How could Joey's foster parents legally change Joey's name without legally adopting him?

Why would the social workers of today care about any blunders that might have been made by a social worker some 30 years ago? I was sure that today's social workers would all side with Patsy.

I decided to try a different approach. I made telephone inquiries to three people residing in the same town where Patsy and Joey had been born. Patsy thought that perhaps people that lived in the same town where she and Joey were born might know the whereabouts of Joey. Perhaps one of those families had become Joey's foster parents. It was my impression after speaking with all three of the neighbours, that they were all terrified of telling anything they might know.

I asked Patsy to send me a letter expressing her feelings about Joey when the two of them were last together at the ages of five and three, and how she has felt being apart from her brother all of these years.

Her letter arrived two months before Christmas. I wrote a Letter to the Editor in the city close to where she and Joey had been born, asking if everyone reading the newspaper would assist in locating Joey. Patsy told about her birth, Joey's birth, that she had been adopted, and how her adoptive parents had tried to adopt Joey so that they could grow up together. She told all about that last day that she and Joey had seen one another and the tears and pain that she has felt since that day.

I titled the newspaper article "A Stick of Gum for Joey." Since the article would appear in their newspaper just before Christmas, the Editor renamed it "All I want for Christmas is to Find my Brother Joey." Before printing the story, the newspaper editor contacted Mr. Gordon of Social Services in order to include his side of the story. It read:

> Social Services stated in a telephone interview that 'because Patsy and Joey did not grow up together in the same home, they are not really brother and sister'.

The article ended with Patsy's feelings and her plea for help to locate her brother Joey:

> Finding out you are adopted is not the hard part. It's the wondering if you have someone of your blood that has some of your same traits, and if each of you smile the same way. You grow up and marry and have a family of your own, but yet you keep open a special corner of your heart for someone you love, but you really don't know who he is or where he is. So... your fairytale begins.

> But as the years go by, you have to turn this dream into reality. Who do you turn to for help? Who will understand? Every Christmas you watch the fantasies and magic in the hearts of your children. You watch your husband share Christmas with his brothers, sisters, nieces and nephews, and you stand back alone – wondering... 'Where is my family? Where is my brother Joey.' You remember an elderly man you spoke with 10 years ago who said your parents are now dead, and you remember replying 'I suppose my little brother has died

as well; and his reply 'Oh No!' Joey is very much alive.' And you wonder 'does this man know where my brother is?'

You wonder if Joey's foster parents know that he has a sister, and you wonder if he has tried to find you. Somehow you feel that they wouldn't mind if you met your brother, and you feel confident. But then you fight the reality of government bureaucracy and the world of government secrecy.

You look into your purse and see that stick of gum – a lingering memory of your brother and you wish 'All I want for Christmas is to put my arms around my little brother and give him a Sister who loves him very much.

The article took up three quarters of page 2 of the newspaper, with a sketch of a little girl about five years old with her arm around a little boy about three years old.

The day that the article appeared in the newspaper, my brother telephoned me to say that people everywhere in that city were talking about it.

About three weeks prior to the article appearing, I had written to five schools in that city, one of which I felt Joey had attended from the age of 6 to 12, telling each principal the story of Patsy searching for her brother Joey, and I asked all of them if they could possibly check their records for a boy who had had his name changed from Joey to some new name in approximately 1952 when he was 10 years old. While I was talking with my own brother, I asked him if he would telephone those five schools to see if he could find out anything. He agreed.

Later that evening my brother telephoned me to say that he had found the right school and that the principal had said to him:

> I will give you Joey's new name if you would promise to phone Joey and ask him if he would like to see his sister. If you agree, I will give you that name in a few days."

My brother agreed to the principal's request. I felt that if we did not have any results from the newspaper article, at least we would find out Joey's new name from the school principal in a day or two.

While waiting, my brother said that he would make an appointment with Mr. Gordon to see if he would tell George anything in person.

About 9:00 a.m. the next morning, my telephone rang. It was Mr. Gordon. He said "Do you know who I just talked to?" I replied "Yes, my brother."

"No!" he said. I just spoke with Joey.

"Joey?" I replied breathlessly. "I can't believe it!."

Mr. Gordon said excitedly, "Well, believe it." Joey evidently told Mr. Gordon that he was thrilled to find out that he has a sister. He said he could not remember her and would therefore probably never have gone searching for her. Mr. Gordon said that he asked Joey if he wanted to meet his sister, and he said, "Of course I do!"

I asked Mr. Gordon, "Did you give Joey Patsy's phone number?"

"Yes," he replied. "I gave him Patsy's phone number where she works at the Legion and at her home. He should be phoning her right now as we speak. Mr. Gordon said that Joey lives in Calgary. His foster sister saw the article in the newspaper yesterday, and she telephoned him and read it to him over the phone last night.

....

Evidently, Joey dialled Patsy's phone number at her home, but there was no answer. He then dialled the phone number for the Legion where she is the manager. As the manager, Patsy is responsible for the running and the maintenance of the Legion.

It had been a stressful morning for Patsy. She had telephoned the plumber many times in the last three days to come and fix the toilet in the men's washroom, which, in the past three days had turned into a small flood. The inconvenience was becoming unbearable for the members.

The telephone rang. Patsy picked up the receiver and said "hello!" The man on the telephone said, "I understand that you have been looking for me?"

Patsy replied sternly, "Where have you been? I have been phoning you every few hours for the past three days. We need you to come here right now and fix the toilet in the men's washroom."

At that point Joey said quietly, "This is your brother Joey!"

Patsy told me that she was shocked and dumbfounded. She didn't know whether to laugh or cry, or to scream in shear delight.

Patsy and Joey talked for over an hour. During that time they made arrangements to meet the next evening in a certain restaurant in Calgary. Patsy told Joey she would be wearing a white suit.

The next evening when Patsy walked into the restaurant, she was not sure if Joey was already there. She stood still, looking all around the restaurant. Finally she spotted a man staring at her. He was fairly stalky with grey hair and a handlebar moustache. As she walked toward him, he stood up. Patsy asked, "Joey?" He replied, "yes!" They stared at one another for a minute or so and then they hugged.

Joey ordered a bottle of wine, and while they were waiting for it, they stared at one another, looking for resemblances. Finally, Patsy said in a choked voice, "Just a minute. I have something for you." She reached into her purse, and yes – it's true. She handed him a stick of gum.

CHAPTER FOUR

AT THE TOP OF
THE WINDING
STAIRCASE

Melanie is a dear friend of mine that lives here in Alberta. She was born in Yarmouth Nova Scotia in the summer of 1950, placed for adoption at four months of age, and adopted by a prominent family soon after. Her adopted father was an Accountant, and her adoptive mother was literally "the wife of an Accountant." After Melanie was adopted, her parents moved to Halifax.

Melanie attended Dalhousie University in Halifax graduating with a degree in nursing. She had difficulty finding a suitable job as a nurse in Nova Scotia and therefore moved to Alberta.

At the age of 29, Melanie made up her mind that she wanted to find her birth mother and birth father. In January of 1980 we wrote a letter to Social Services in Halifax, requesting information about her birth parents. We also requested a copy of her Adoption Order hoping that her birth name would appear on it.

Three months passed before Melanie received a reply to her request. The Adoption Co-ordinator, Miss Finch, replied – stating that at the time of Melanie's birth, her mother was 23 years of age, single, born in Canada, was a bookkeeper, of Scottish origin, and her birth mother had one sister still living at home. Melanie's birth father was 28 years old, married, was a policeman, and was also of Scottish origin. The letter went on to state that Melanie's birth name was "identifying" information and it was therefore the policy in Nova Scotia that biological surnames not appear on Adoption Orders. However, Miss Finch stated that she would have a social worker contact Melanie's birth mother to see if she would be interested in meeting Melanie.

Two months went by with no reply. In the next six months, each time Melanie wrote to Miss Finch, she always responded, "I have not as yet heard from the Social Worker who was going to contact your birth mother, but will advise you upon receipt of information from her."

Finally Melanie decided to telephone Miss Finch, but each time she did, Miss Finch was in a meeting. Due to the time difference between Alberta and Nova Scotia, Melanie started phoning Miss Finch at 5:00 a.m. Alberta time in order to try to reach Miss Finch at 9:00 a.m. Nova Scotia time. It took three telephone calls to finally speak to her by telephone. Miss Finch simply repeated, "I have not as yet heard from the Social Worker, etc....." Miss Finch had the same reply to telephone inquiries made during the next four months.

Melanie and I decided that – rather than write any more letters or place any more telephone calls, we would fly to Halifax and visit Miss Finch in person. However, we did ensure in a special delivery registered letter to Miss Finch that she knew of our arrival. We were hoping that Miss Finch would make a special effort to contact the Social Worker, who may hopefully also arrange for Melanie to meet her birth mother while we were there.

Melanie's birthday was August 3rd. When we boarded the plane on July 25th, I said to Melanie, "Wouldn't it be nice if you could spend your birthday with your birth mother?"

It wasn't long before Melanie was sound asleep curled up in a tight little ball on the seat next to me. I stared at her long blonde hair, parted in the middle. She had never tried a new hair style the whole while that I knew her. She said that women who repeatedly changed their hairstyles and fashions must be bored with their lives and needed to fill some sort of void in their lives. Melanie said she did not feel any type of void in her life, and yet, here she was on a plane flying across the country to hopefully meet the woman who gave birth to her. I was not sure if this was just Melanie's personality, or if it was the disposition of most people born on the east coast.

Melanie was a quiet person, never allowing anyone to know what she was thinking or feeling and was rarely involved in open discussions on any topic. I had thought that she had often put up a wall between herself and the other nurses and patients at the hospital where she worked. I wondered, as I stared at her, just how emotional she would be if she met her birth mother. That could be interesting!

Having landed at our destination, we had a rental car waiting. Since Melanie had lived in Nova Scotia for most of her life, she knew the way to her Grandmother's house, which would be our home for the next week. I was delighted that we were only a short distance from a harbour.

We drove to the Government building that evening, which was set apart from the rest of the City. The building was a boring clay colour and the grounds were vast and empty of trees and flowers. We stopped the car and stared.

Melanie uttered, "Somewhere in that building that looks like an institution – is my file; a file with my name in it and the names of my birth mother and my birth father. If only I could walk right in there, put my file under my coat and walk out." I felt sure that many adoptees would feel the same way. Stealing her file would have been nice at the time, however, we would never have had the exciting experiences and adventures that awaited us in the next seven days.

The next morning Melanie and I drove to the Government building, walked up to the second floor and asked for Miss Finch. We imagined from her name that she might be fairly short, small boned and would have mousey brown untidy hair. Our premonition was accurate.

"Come in Melanie," she said nonchalantly, as though Melanie had simply walked across the street rather than flown across the country. Thinking that Miss Finch may divulge more information to Melanie if I were not in the room, I left them alone and went downstairs to the basement coffee room.

An hour later, Melanie joined me and we talked for only a few minutes. Miss Finch had simply reiterated the information given to Melanie in the very first letter, "Your mother was unwed at the time of your birth. She relinquished you for adoption at four months of age. Your mother lived at the Shadybrook Home for Unwed Mothers in Yarmouth from the time she was six months pregnant up until your relinquishment for adoption when you were four months old. Your mother was a bookkeeper, with a Grade 12 education. She was 5 ft. 5 inches in height, with blonde hair and blue eyes. She was 23 years of age at the time of your birth. Your father was a policeman of Scottish origin. He was married at the time of your birth. He was 28 years of age, with dark hair and brown eyes. Your birth mother and father's relationship had lasted four years, and at the time of your adoption they were still seeing one another."

Melanie said "I wonder why she put me up for adoption if they were still seeing one another?"

In the next few hours we played the "What If..." game that most adoptees play:

"What if he couldn't leave his wife for some strange or awful reason, but loved your mother very much?"

"What if she tried to keep you, but found after four months it was impossible – and why four months?"

"What if she didn't tell your birth father that she had his baby – but then – we resolved that question when we were told that they were still seeing one another when Melanie was placed for adoption at four months of age."

"What if you were taken from your birth mother against her will?"

Sandra Butler Ladwig

We pondered whether or not Melanie's adopted father knew anything about her birth parents that he was not saying. Melanie told me that she had written to her adoptive father advising him that she had started a search for her birth mother. His reply very simply stated, "I love you as though you were my own daughter. Is that not enough for you? Your mother loved you too right up to the day she died." Melanie told me that her adoptive mother died of a brain tumour when Melanie was seven years old."

The next day we went back to the Government to see Miss Finch. I had suggested to Melanie that she say something to Miss Finch to the effect that we would not be staying in Nova Scotia for any more than four days, and what a shame not to spend the remaining few days with her birth mother and possibly meet her birth father. Again I went down to the basement coffee room.

In about 15 minutes Melanie came down to the coffee room, and since she seemed impatient, we left. While we were driving away, from the look on Melanie's face, I kept silent. Finally she said, "Miss Finch told me she would try to contact the social worker today. I am to phone her back in two days."

We told Grandmother that we were driving to Yarmouth that afternoon and would not be back for two days. On our road trip to Yarmouth, it was wonderful to see all of the fishing villages along the various coastlines and the "Cook Lobster While You Wait" stands along the highway. I wanted to stop at every one of them and get sick of Lobster, if that could ever happen to anyone.

Without a birth name to go on, it was difficult to go

to the various Churches in Yarmouth to search through Baptismal records, but we did in fact visit the old Church that Melanie and her father had attended. While there, we did speak with the Minister. I wondered if Melanie would bring up the subject of her birth and adoption. After the Minister left, she said that she was afraid that he might think her to be ungrateful to her minister father by searching for her birth parents. Before we left the Church, we took photographs of one another high up in the pulpit, with our arms wavering hell and damnation – just like in the movie Pollyanna. Those photographs would some day go into Melanie's memoirs.

Melanie explained to me that her adopted father was a powerful man who had a need to control those around him. He always monopolized every conversation. Melanie said that nobody in the family had an identity of their own. Everybody was described by their relationship to her father John.

I found this to be true the next day when we visited Melanie's mother's grave. The inscription on the headstone read, "In Loving Memory of John Black's wife, Hazel." Nearby was a grave that John had purchased for Melanie. She said she would imagine what the inscription might be, "Here lies John Black's daughter – Melanie!"

"Here – take my picture," Melanie said, as she laid down on top of her grave with her arms stretched out. "This is the only property I own in the world," she giggled. Nothing doing – it was then my turn. I had to lie down on Melanie's property to get my photograph taken! I could only imagine what my inscription might say.

We approached the Shadybrook Home for Unwed

Mothers; the Home where Melanie and her mother had lived together for four months. It was a two-storey L-shaped building with soft yellow siding. At one end there was a small brook with wild flowers growing all around. Rose bushes were in full bloom all along the front of the building.

We got out of our car and walked into the Home. The people sitting in a large sun room seemed to be senior citizens. We walked down a hallway and spoke with a nurse, who wore the name tag Mrs. McGregor. Melanie explained who she was and why she was visiting the Home.

Mrs. McGregor was a delightful woman, short, plump and middle-aged. She said that she had worked in the Home for many years, even when it had been a Home for Unwed Mothers. "It's a shame that those records are no longer here," she said. "I would sure like to look up your information and give it to you."

We asked Mrs. McGregor if she could show us around the building. "Only too pleased," she replied. As we walked – she talked. "Girls giving birth to babies who stayed in this Home had to keep their babies for four months. After that time, they were to decide whether to keep their babies or relinquish them for adoption. Each girl was requested to stay the entire four months in order that she be sure of her decision." Now Melanie understood why her mother had kept her for four months.

As Mrs. McGregor walked toward a wide, long winding staircase going up to the second floor, she said, "Quite often we had a birth mother standing up there at the top of these stairs holding her baby, with the adopting parents waiting down here at the bottom. A nurse would simply go up the stairs, take the baby from the birth mother, walk down the winding staircase and then hand the baby to his or her new parents here at the bottom. With the way the staircase winds, one parent could never see the other!"

We asked Mrs. McGregor if we could go upstairs. "Of course" she said. "I'll come with you." We walked up the long staircase to the top.

Mrs. McGregor said, "the rooms have been changed around a little bit, but basically they are much the same."

Melanie and I walked past each doorway wondering which room she and her mother had lived in for four months. We stared into each room as though looking for a clue – something that may have been scratched into the wood on the windowsill, still showing through the new paint. Would a birth mother ever think that her daughter may return some day – looking for a clue? a name? It's strange how one romanticizes the reality of many years ago.

On the way down the staircase I stepped ahead and asked if I could take a photograph of Mrs. McGregor and Melanie half way down the stairs. At the last minute I wanted to yell at Melanie, "Jump into her arms!" However, I snapped their picture and then another at the bottom. The picture at the top of the winding staircase would remain blank for the moment.

After thanking Mrs. McGregor, Melanie and I walked outside. Melanie began to stroll toward the brook. I walked the other direction around the building in order to leave her alone for a while. I imagined that Melanie was thinking that her mother had likely carried her out to the brook several times during their four months together.

After about half an hour I walked back around the front of the building. I could see Melanie over by the brook picking flowers. She saw me standing by the building and started to walk toward me while gazing at the front of the Home. As we came together, she said, "I wonder if we could come back in the middle of the night, dig up some of those rose bushes and put them under the seat of our plane ride home. We both laughed as we walked back to the car.

The next morning we drove around Yarmouth and finally decided to go to the Court House there. At the counter we asked the clerk if we could get a copy of Melanie's birth records. After leaving us there for about ten minutes, the clerk came back and then scolded Melanie for even asking for such a thing. She bluntly said, "Those adoption records are sealed." Melanie said she felt as though she was a criminal.

At the end of the day we found a nice motel, making sure that our room had a television set so that we could watch the Royal Wedding between Princess Diana and Prince Charles. There was a knock at the door at 5:00 a.m., with breakfast on trays fit for two Queens. We propped our pillows, turned on the television and enjoyed the fine performance of the Royal Wedding.

Later that morning we drove to Melanie's house where she had lived for ten years.

"Would you like to go inside?" I asked Melanie.

"No!" she replied grumpily, with no further explanation.

Melanie said that there was a lady named Jean who had been best friends with her adoptive mother. We decided to try to find Jean and visit with her. We found her house and knocked on her door. After announcing our identity, Jean was thrilled to meet Melanie and she invited us in for tea. All during the preparation and much to my amazement, Melanie talked non-stop. Everything that could possibly hit her brain in that two hour period came out of her mouth. When she finished talking about herself she began talking about me. I realized what Melanie was up to, but I wasn't convinced that it would work. Then she came directly to the point.

"Do you know anything about my adoption?" Melanie asked. I looked at Jean. There was silence in the room. I was thinking, "If only she knew Melanie's birth name," but Jean remained silent for a long time. Then she said, "I remember when your mother and father adopted you, but I didn't know anything about your birth. Your mother and I were good friends and I was sorry to hear about her death when you were only a child."

I silently thought, "If Jean knew anything about Melanie's birth, she wasn't about to share her well-guarded secret with Melanie." After we left Jean's house we drove around wondering if Melanie's birth mother had lived in Yarmouth, and perhaps still lives here. Could she have been contacted by a social worker this very day?

When we headed back down the highway to Halifax, we wondered if her birth mother might live on the western coastline of Nova Scotia. There had to be some reason why Miss Finch and the social worker in question could not connect easily. Another thing – if her birth mother agreed to meet Melanie, would she have to drive clear across the province to meet her? Then we concluded that – for sure the social worker must live far away from the government buildings in Halifax – otherwise it wouldn't be taking so long.

We headed back to Halifax in order to meet Miss Finch the next day.

On the way back, our game of "What if..." "Would she..." "Did she...." – made our trip back go quickly. We arrived in Halifax quite late and therefore decided to stay in a hotel rather than wake up Melanie's grandmother. In the middle of the night Melanie woke up screaming because of a nightmare she had. I am sure it was because of all of the emotions of the previous day.

The next morning over breakfast, we talked about Melanie's birth father being a policeman. I had an idea. I phoned the Police Department and spoke with a policeman who gave me the names of two policemen from the 1950 era. I telephoned the first one and explained who I was and why I was calling.

"Now, let me think." he replied. "I seem to recall there was a man who one might describe that way. No! No! I can't remember his name, but I remember his face. He was quite a man with the ladies."

Silently I thought, "I don't want someone who was quite a man with the ladies. I want a man who was quite a man with only one lady."

I contemplated what kind of a man her birth father

was. Why did he date Melanie's mother if he was married? Why did their relationship last four years or more if he was married. Didn't he love his wife? And if not – why didn't he love his wife? If he loved his wife, how could he date Melanie's mother? Was his wife crippled or sick? If he loved Melanie's mother, why didn't he divorce his wife, marry Melanie's mother and keep their baby?

When we drove over to Grandmother's house in the morning, Melanie telephoned Miss Finch. I could see that she was nervous. When she hung up, she turned toward me and said, with a smile on her face, "Miss Finch said that when my mother was first approached, she was hesitant. However, she has finally agreed to meet me. Miss Finch said she is not sure whether this will be a happy event for my mother or not." Melanie seemed disappointed and a little edgy. I know from all of our discussions this past year, Melanie had hoped that her mother would accept her with open arms. Miss Finch's message wasn't exactly, "open arms!"

Melanie went on to say, "I am supposed to telephone Miss Finch back in the morning at her home since its Saturday, and she will give me a time and place where I am to meet my mother."

From that moment on – all through that day, Melanie was far off in a world of her own. She had put that brick wall back up again.

She and I went shopping for a new outfit for Melanie to wear when she was to meet her mother. We went from store to store where Melanie tried on several dresses, however, they either did not fit properly, or they were the wrong colour. We left the mall empty-handed. On the drive back to Grandmother's house, Melanie was quiet and distant.

"Listen Melanie," I said, "Your mother is probably very excited to meet you, and has dreamed of this moment for years." (I was not sure that I had convinced Melanie or not.)

That night we went to a restaurant on the Harbour overlooking the ships. I tried to be positive. "Do you know Melanie, that right now, at this very moment, your birth mother knows that you are here in Halifax! She knows you are here to meet her! Think of how she feels and what she is thinking." Melanie giggled and then she laughed out loud. Her positive mood was finally delightful.

All of the letters, the phone calls, the months and months of frustration, the visits to Miss Finch's office, the thoughts by the brook, the contemplations while driving across the province – they were all worth it now. Her mother knew Melanie was here!

There was one other couple sitting in the restaurant. The lady stared and stared at Melanie. After a while it became very obvious to Melanie too. "Could that be her?" I said quietly. "While you are wondering about her, is that her right over there wondering about you?" The woman continued to stare and stare, not saying anything to her own dinner companion.

"I'm going to go over to the salad bar and I will stay there for a while," I said. "Let's see if she comes over to you." I took my salad plate and walked down to the other end of the restaurant to the salad bar. I took my time choosing as I watched out the side of my eye. The woman did not budge. I took long enough that if she were going to go over to Melanie, she had plenty of opportunity. I finally walked back to our table.

Then we played our game again. "Did she have to drive across the province?" "Is she on her way here now?" "Is she coming tomorrow?" "Does she in fact live right here in Halifax?" Thinking that through, we concluded that she must live far away, otherwise why would Miss Finch engage the services of another social worker?" She must live far enough away that Miss Finch could not contact her herself.

The next morning Melanie telephoned Miss Finch at her home. Miss Finch told Melanie to come to her house at 2:00 o'clock that afternoon and her birth mother would be there waiting to meet her. From the address given, Miss Finch lives only three blocks from Grandmother's house.

Melanie telephoned a hairdresser and made an appointment to have her hair done. I stayed with Grandmother. We sat in the back yard in the sunlight. Since it was August 2nd and tomorrow would be Melanie's birthday, I went to the Mall and purchased a gold ring for Melanie with an August birthstone in the centre.

At noon, Melanie returned home. Her blonde hair hung down perfectly straight, and shone like a mirror in the sunlight. It was very beautiful. We had lunch ready for her, but she was too nervous to eat anything. The three of us sat at the table in the kitchen, but as Grandmother and I talked, Melanie sat silently – far off in thought. Then I remembered. I reached into my purse and brought out the birthstone ring. I handed it to her and said "I know it's not your birthday until tomorrow, but I want you to have this today. Whenever you look at it, I want you to remember this very day."

Melanie reached over and hugged me, and then I put the ring on her finger.

"Well, I better get ready now," Melanie said, giving herself almost an hour.

When she came upstairs she looked lovely, dressed in a pink linen dress, with white shoes and white purse. Grandmother and I walked her out to the car, where we saw a beautiful flowering plant sitting in the back seat.

Both Grandmother and I kissed Melanie, wished her luck, and told her we would be thinking of nothing else but her while she was gone. She got into the car, backed out of the driveway and she drove off down the street.

Waiting for Melanie would have been very difficult for Grandmother and me, except for the fact that we got busy and planned a very special dinner for Melanie – lobster, baked potatoes, veggies, a Black Forest Cake, and wine. We had just finished preparing dinner when the back door opened and Melanie walked in – with a bounce in her step.

"Hi!" she said excitedly. She was all smiles.

"Let's all get comfortable at the table, and then we'll talk," her Grandmother said.

Patience is a virtue I find with most east coast Canadian people. Grandmother seated herself at the head of the table, with Melanie on one side and me on the other. Lobster was a wonderful new experience for me. Grandmother gave each of us a bib and crackers, and took pictures of the two of us holding up our Lobsters.

When we were all finished, I poured a second glass of wine, and then Grandmother and I sat silently in anticipation as we listened to Melanie.

"Well," she said, with a grin, "I will start at the very beginning. First I got to Miss Finch's house. There was a barricade over the front door, so I had to walk to the back door. Miss Finch greeted me, wearing old black pedal-pusher pants with splatters of paint all over them, and she was barefooted. I found her attire rather odd for a woman in your profession. However, she led me up into her kitchen which looked like it was in the middle of renovations.

"Your mother is in the living room," she said. "Go right in and I'll bring some tea." She pointed down a small hallway.

"I could feel my heart pounding more than ever as I walked down the hallway and turned into the living room. Standing across the room by the fireplace was a woman about 5 ft. 5 inches, blonde hair, with a very slim figure. She was wearing a navy suit with a white collar. I stared at her – speechless! She turned around and looked at me. We just stared at one another for a few moments and then we lunged toward one another. We both hugged and then cried in each other's arms. When Miss Finch came into the room with a tray of tea and cookies, we stood back from one another. Miss Finch introduced us properly.

"My mother's name is Eve McDonald. We sat across from one another, politely taking sips from our tea. Miss Finch led the conversation after that – mostly small talk. I didn't know if my mother wanted to leave as much as I

Sandra Butler Ladwig

did. I wanted to have her all to myself, some place away from that house and away from Miss Finch.

"When the time came that it was polite to leave, we thanked Miss Finch for opening up her home to us, and we walked out the back door together.

"Eve suggested we go to her house. I was so pleased to finally find out where she lives. I followed closely behind Eve until we arrived at her house. When we both got out of our cars we stood together in front of her house. I had dreamt of this moment for most of my life.

"I was trying to get up the nerve to ask her what my name was. Finally I said, 'Was my last name McDonald too?.'

"No, she replied, 'your full name was Debra Ann Anderson.'

"Anderson? Can you imagine that. You wouldn't think that Anderson would have been such a difficult name to guess. Then Eve took me into her home."

Melanie looked straight at me. She said, "Wait until I tell you where she lives. When we dined last night at the harbour, if we had walked outside and yelled her name, she would have heard us because she lives only about half a block away from that restaurant."

Melanie looked at me and we both laughed. "Across the province, bah!," and we both laughed again.

"Well then," Melanie continued. "Once inside of Eve's home I could see photographs on her piano that were wedding pictures and family group photos. I was afraid to ask who they were. Eve stood behind me and pointed out who each person was in the photographs.

Your father, Nelson and I married three years ago. This is our wedding picture.'

"I was so excited to hear that she had married my father. While she was still pointing at the wedding picture, she told me that Nelson's wife had been in a mental institution since long before I was born. He didn't want to divorce her, out of respect for his wife and their children. They both decided to wait until Nelson's wife died and then get married, which was only four years ago. Then Eve pointed out a photograph of Nelson's daughter who looks just like me and Nelson's two sons and their families.

"Eve asked me to sit down, and she went into the kitchen to make some lemonade. When she came back into the room we sat across from one another. There were so many things I wanted to ask her, but I didn't want to pry into her life. Finally, Eve just started talking. She told me that she and my father loved one another very much at the time I was conceived, and have loved one another ever since. She explained that, at the time I was born, her parents refused to help her, and she couldn't see how she could work and raise a baby too. Eve said that she didn't want Nelson to feel forced into divorcing his wife and marrying her and so she told Nelson that she had decided to put me up for adoption.

"She said that she thought at the time that her decision might have been a relief for him because he was pulled so strongly in two different directions. Eve told me that if she had wanted Nelson to divorce his wife, she knew he would have. She said she was so worried that the rest of the family might hate him for that and hate her and their baby Debra as well.

"She told me that when I was 18 years old, she and Nelson hoped that some day I would come looking for them. Even though it took several more years than they had hoped for, they were both so happy that I eventually came looking for them.

Looking at both Grandmother and I, Melanie said, "I was confused when she said that, so I asked her, 'If you married my father four years ago, and if you loved me and wanted to see me, then why were you hesitant about meeting me when the social worker came to see you'?

"Eve looked baffled at my question. Then she added, 'I wasn't hesitant about meeting you? I was thrilled.' Then she uttered, 'Oh, I know what you mean. The day the social worker came to see me, she rang my doorbell, and when I answered the door, she blurted out – 'Are you the Eve McDonald who gave birth to a baby in August of 1950 and gave her up for adoption?' Eve said she just stared at the social worker in disbelief, and then she opened the door wide so that the social worker could see the eight ladies from Eve's church that were seated in her living room. They had all heard every word that the social worker had asked. The social worker must have known I was shocked and embarrassed because she whispered – 'I'm sorry – I didn't mean to intrude,' and then she left.

Back at Grandmother's house, Melanie reiterated, "So you see – my mother wasn't hesitant about meeting me at all. She was just shocked over the manner in which she had been approached.

"Remembering back to the months of letters and

phone calls, Melanie questioned Eve why it had taken so long to finally arrange a meeting? Eve again looked baffled. Then she replied, 'the social worker came to see me only two days ago. It was only yesterday that I telephoned Miss Finch and found out that you were here in Halifax.'

"Can you believe that?" Melanie stated as she snapped her fingers. "Can you believe it? Two days ago!

"I told Eve all about the letters and telephone calls during the past year and a half, and she was annoyed."

I then asked Melanie, "What about your father – Nelson? Are you going to get an opportunity to meet him?"

Melanie said that Eve was going to pick her up in the morning and have her come to her house to meet her father Nelson. She confirmed that Nelson was as excited to meet Melanie as she was, but that he thought it would be wonderful if they spent a day alone together.

Melanie slept well that night. The next morning she got up, dressed and she very excitedly waited for Eve to pick her up. Grandmother and I watched through the curtains when Eve pulled up, Melanie ran out, and they drove off.

When Melanie came back late that afternoon, we all sat down while she told us all about Nelson. She remarked, "He is a wonderful person – young at heart, jovial, and very Scottish. Melanie stated that when she watched Eve and Nelson together, it was like looking at two teenage lovers, always considerate of one another. It is a wonderful thing anywhere in the world when a child of any age sees his or her parents so much in love.

Melanie was delighted that she was the result of that love.

Melanie and I had to fly home the next day. Eve asked if she and Nelson could drive us to the airport. I was thrilled, because I would finally meet both of them too.

The next morning, we dropped our car off at the car rental office downtown, and when we walked outside, Eve and Nelson were waiting. We went over to their car and got in. Melanie introduced me to Eve and Nelson, and when I looked at Eve, she was exactly as I had envisioned her to be, petite and beautiful.

We started to drive toward the Airport, and as we approached the Shadybrook Home, I asked Eve and Melanie if they would mind stopping by for a few minutes. They both looked at one another, smiled, and said "sure!" I was hoping to sneak a few pictures of Melanie, Eve and Nelson in front of the Home. I knew Melanie would cherish those photographs forever.

Nelson parked their car at the front of the Home by the rose bushes. When we got out of the car, Eve, Nelson and Melanie walked toward the brook, where I took a few pictures of them together. Then I said, "There's a picture of the two of you together that I would like to take." Nelson decided to stay in the car.

Eve said, "Just lead the way."

"Follow me," I motioned, as we walked into the Home, through the sun room, and up to the top of the winding staircase. I stopped, but Eve continued on down the hallway to the room where she and Melanie had lived together. When she turned around, she smiled at Melanie and said, "This was our room."

Melanie smiled back at her. Then Eve whispered, "I remember so many of the girls who lived here with us. At one time I remember how the mother and her baby would stand at the top of the stairs there, and a nurse would come and take the baby from her and walk down the stairs and hand the baby to the new parents. Two or three of the girls would go outside and get the license number of the car belonging to the adopting parents. Then we would give it to the mother so that she could find out who they were and where they lived. If they lived in Halifax or close by, the mothers could watch her child grow up if she wanted to. Then one day the girls were caught writing down the license number, and that was the end of that. From then on, a man named Norbert would come and take the baby to another building."

As the three of us walked back toward the top of the stairs, I ran on ahead and took a picture of Melanie and Eve at the top of the winding staircase, and a few more as they walked down the stairs to the bottom – hand in hand.

Melanie has been back to Halifax to visit Eve and Nelson several times since that first meeting. No mention has ever been made of Melanie meeting Nelson's children. However, she just secretly smiles, realizing that she is the result of a very special love.

CHAPTER FIVE

LOVE IS BORN IN THE HEART – NOT UNDER IT

My twin brother George and I were born at Killam Alberta in 1941. In our late teens and early twenties we both believed that we were adopted. We never did talk about it to one another nor to our parents. I don't know what it was that led us to believe that we were adopted. During our growing up years "adoption" was a dirty word. It meant that nobody wanted you. The kids at school bullied me and were mean to me – possibly because of my freckles and red hair. They called me "Carrot Top." Nobody was mean to George. He was not afraid of anybody or anything and was very popular racing stock cars.

However, at the age of 26 both my brother and I wanted to find out about our birth family or families. Maybe we weren't even twins. I went to the hospital where we were born and asked to see our birth records, but the young girl there told me that she could not bring our records to the front desk.

One day we went to talk to our Granny Hodam and

asked her to tell us all about our birth families and our adoption.

I am sure that Granny could see that we were convinced that we were adopted. She said, "You were not adopted, but your Mother was, but she doesn't know it."

Granny went on to explain that when she and Grampa went back to Nebraska to visit relatives in 1915, on their way back to Alberta they stopped at the Florence Criettien Home for Unwed Mothers in Sioux City Iowa to possibly adopt a baby. Granny and Grampa talked about adopting a baby boy who could some day work on the farm and then inherit their farm. Granny said that once they were inside the Home, they were taken to an office where the matron brought out a beautiful little baby girl all dressed in pink. Granny said that they held her for a few minutes, but then the matron said, "Just wait a minute. I have a little baby that needs a home very badly." The matron brought out Mom, who was wearing only a diaper and a night shirt. Granny said that her heart went out to that little baby girl and she said to Grampa, "this little baby needs a home as badly as we need a baby."

Since Granny and Grampa were unable to get a birth certificate for Mom before they left the Home, Granny fed Mom, put her to sleep in a suitcase sitting in the back seat, and at the border she simply lowered the lid of the suitcase and snapped it shut. When the border guard asked if they had anything to declare, they said "No." Once over the border, Granny unsnapped the suitcase and lifted the lid. Then they were off to Alberta to a town called Strome where they had previously homesteaded a section of land. Grampa (called "Doc" by everyone) was the veterinarian in the county. Months later, Granny received a birth certificate for Mom, showing her adopted name as Helen Louise Hodam born on September 27, 1915 in Sioux City Iowa. It showed her parents as Edna and George Hodam.

When George and I were 26 years old, we had a long talk with Granny, who told us all about our mother's birth and adoption. Both George and I persuaded Granny to tell Mom all about her adoption. Granny confided that she had told Dad about Mom's adoption before they were married because of the stigma around adoption. Dad, bless his soul, said that it made no difference to him. He said that he loved Mom because of the wonderful person she was.

About two weeks after our chat with Granny, she and Dad told Mom all about her birth and subsequent adoption. At first Mom said that she felt that Granny and Grampa had really wanted the first little baby girl back at the Home but then Granny convinced Mom that she was "chosen" because she was special. Mom said that she now knew why the girls at her school on the farm had bullied her and called her a bastard.

Granny, on the other hand, said to Mom, "Well now that you know the truth, you have a family and I have no one."

In 1942 during the War, Mom, Dad, George and I moved from Strome to Bonnie Doon in Edmonton where Dad worked for Aircraft Repair. Granny and Grampa missed all of us so much so they sold the farm and moved to Edmonton. They bought the house across the lane from our house. In the years to follow, Mom waited on Granny and Grampa hand and foot, cleaning and cooking for them every day. Mom said, "I owe them my life."

Many years later after Granny and Grampa had both died, Mom decided that she wanted to find her birth mother. I had a copy of my Mother's adoption papers, which showed her Mother's birth mother's name as "Dora Kistenmacher."

I phoned the long distance operator for Sioux City Iowa asking for any listing for the name "Kistenmacher." There was none. Since I was allowed to ask for only three towns or cities at a time, I asked for two close-by towns in Iowa, but again, there was no one by that surname.

Then, thinking that a birth mother, wanting to give birth to her baby and give her up for adoption in total secrecy, may be from a nearby state, I checked the atlas to see all states that surrounded Iowa. I telephoned the operator asking for three towns in the state of South Dakota. On the third town, which was Clark, South Dakota, the operator gave me the phone number of a "William Kistenmacher."

I dialled the phone number for William Kistenmacher in Clark, South Dakota, and the man that answered said that he was William. I fabricated my reason for wanting to reach Dora Kistenmacher saying, "I would like to contact Dora Kistenmacher on behalf of my Grandmother Edna Hodam, who went to school with Dora many years ago." William said that Dora had married and she was now Dora Kretzschmar living at Willow Lake. He gave me Dora's phone number. I thanked William and was then very pleased that I had finally found my Mother's birth mother. (20 minutes)

Later that day, after my children were sleeping, I phoned Dora Kretzschmar in Willow Lake, South Dakota. I did not want to talk to Dora directly out of fear of giving her a heart attack. A lady by the name of Margie answered the phone.

I said, "My name is Sandra Butler. I live in Alberta Canada. My mother was born at the Florence Crittien Home in Sioux City Iowa. My grandmother, Dora Kistenmacher, gave birth to my mother at the Florence Crittien Home in Sioux City Iowa in September of 1915 and Dora then placed my mother for adoption. Shortly after my mother's birth she was adopted by George and Edna Hodam and was then taken from Iowa to Alberta Canada where she grew up on a farm. Mom would very much like to meet her mother Dora."

Margie said, "I'm sorry. Could you please repeat that again?" I repeated what I had said earlier. Then Margie said that she would have to talk to her brother about this and that she would get back to me in a few days. I gave Margie my phone number.

I phoned my Mom in Edmonton and told her all about finding her birth mother Dora. I told Mom the conversation I had with Margie. Mom said that it would be difficult for her to wait a few days. The next day Mom phoned Margie and emphasized how very much she wanted to meet her mother in person. Mom phoned me and told me that she had a long conversation with Margie. Mom decided that she was going to fly down to the closest big city to Willow Lake. Of course I did not want my mother to go to Willow Lake alone. I found a babysitter for my three small children and then drove up to Edmonton. Knowing that my brother George was coming in from South America at midnight, I went out to the airport to greet him. I told him all about finding Mom's birth mother Dora and Mom's decision to fly to South Dakota to meet her birth mother later that day.

To make a long story short, my twin brother George went to South Dakota with Mom.

When George and Mom came back home, George told me that their plane had landed in Sioux Falls, South Dakota. He and Mom were picked up at the airport and were driven to a farm about 3 hours north. Arriving at a farm, they were taken into a farmhouse and then into the living room where an elderly lady sat in a rocking chair. Someone took Mom over to the lady and introduced Mom, saying, "this is your daughter Evelyn." The lady reached out her hand and shook hands with Mom, saying, "pleased to meet you."

Then Mom and George were introduced to everyone else. There were so many people at the farm that day that neither Mom nor George could remember all of their names. However, it turned out that nine of them were Mom's full brothers and sisters. The others were spouses, cousins, nieces and nephews. Evidently many of Mom's relatives flew in from all over the United States just to meet her.

That afternoon and the days that followed, George was told that – when Dora found out that she was pregnant, she was taken to the Florence Crittien Home in Sioux City Iowa where she would stay until her baby was born. When Mom was born, Dora gave Mom up for adoption and then returned home to Willow Lake. Her boyfriend Carl Kretzschmar went to see Dora and asked her, "Is it true that you had our baby?" Dora replied, "yes." Then Carl said, "Let's get married and go back to the Home and get our baby back." Evidently Dora was delighted and agreed.

They were married at Willow Lake the following Saturday and on Monday they went back to the Florence Crittien Home to get Mom back. Once at the Home, they were sad to hear that their baby had been adopted only three days before. It was said that Dora was sad, but William was devastated. In the years that followed, evidently Dora lost three babies and then she had nine, four of whom were twins.

George went on to say that one day while visiting, Mom went into Dora's bedroom, sat opposite her, and asked, "I have an album here of photographs of me as a baby, in my teens and in my 20's. Would you like to see them?" Dora replied "No, I don't think so!"

Another conversation George had with Mom's sister Margie, was that – after I spoke to Margie on the telephone, she phoned her twin brother Don. Both evidently agreed that it would safer for them to take Dora to the doctor and in his office they would ask their Mother about giving birth to her baby Evelyn.

Once in the doctor's office Don asked Dora, "Is it true that you had a baby back in 1915 and put her up for adoption?" Dora very simply replied, "yes!" Then they asked Dora if she would like to meet her daughter Evelyn. She had evidently replied, "Yes, that would be nice." Dora did not appear to be shocked, upset or excited. Dora did say that Carl was very proud of his nine children, but he had said, "I am just sad about the one that got away."

Just before Mom and George left Willow Lake, a photograph was taken of Dora with her ten children. Everyone in the photograph had auburn hair and they all had freckles just like George and I do.

George brought back a listing of all of the medical problems in Dora and Carl's families, which is very important for all adoptees to know. They are: cancer (which my daughter and I have had), diabetes (that George has), heart problems and leg ulcers, which Mom and I have.

In the year 2018, I can tell you that Carl died in 1956, Dora died at age 83, Mom died at age 87, and George and I are still here at age 77.

After our first visit to meet Dora, we were told that she very generously changed her Will to include Mom. George and I thanked the family for their kindness, but on Mom's behalf we declined their offer because Mom had received the inheritance that her own parents had left her.

Dora crocheted an end-table runner for George, one for Mom and one for me. One of Mom's sisters said that we should all be impressed because Dora had never given one to any of her children or grandchildren. That was a nice gesture.

Our families have gone to Clark and Willow Lake a few times and the Kretzschmar families have been up here to Alberta half a dozen times. To this day, we are all very good friends.

Sandra Butler Ladwig

I had an extra DNA kit last year and followed the instructions. In only 8 weeks I received the results. One was a first cousin Chris who lives in New Jersey. After going over all of the surnames we could think of, I said, "Kretzschmar."

Chris replied, "that is my Grandmother's name." His grandmother and my grandmother were sisters.

Not to take away the very loving friendships that Mom, George and I all have with the Kistenmacher and Kretzschmar families, both George and I agree that "love is born in the heart – not under it." Our grandmother Edna Hodam needs to know that we are all definitely her family.

CHAPTER SIX

PANDORA'S BOX

I believe that a child is born "in the heart" and not under it and because of my belief, I feel that adoptive parents should be shown the respect and consideration of being given the opportunity to support and encourage their adopted child in a search for his or her birth parents. I feel that the understanding and trust between them will bring them closer together, creating a healthy basis upon which to bring into their lives the friendship of a new found birth family.

Certainly it has always been my intention that the hours of hard work involved in finding a birth mother (and birth father) should bring about happiness to everyone involved. If I ever thought that the assistance I provide to adoptees would ever bring pain and suffering to anyone, I would not have even considered being involved.

One day I received a telephone call from an adoptee by the name of Cheryl. She requested my assistance in a search for her birth mother and birth father. Since she did not have any information about them, I dictated a letter to her over the telephone wherein she would request background information from Social Services & Child Welfare on her birth mother and birth father. We also requested a copy of Cheryl's Adoption Order which would contain her birth name, which would likely be the same surname as her birth mother.

I asked Cheryl, "How do your parents feel about you searching for your birth parents?"

She replied. "My mother and father are very elderly. My mother is 86 years old and Dad is 89. They would never understand nor would they ever agree to this."

"Have you ever discussed your adoption with them?" I asked.

"My mother told me when I was 15 years old that I was adopted, but she has never spoken about it since. It wasn't a shock finding out that I was adopted. Somehow I had always felt a bond between me and someone else. Maybe part of it is the fact that my adopted mother has never shown any affection toward me, and yet, I know I have felt affection from someone at one time or another. It's for that reason that I have to find out the truth about my birth."

I asked Cheryl, "Would you ever consider talking to your parents about your adoption and how they would feel if you searched for your birth mother?"

She replied. "I know that my mother would never agree. She would never forgive me for even thinking about it. Another thing – she is very ill right now, and I wouldn't want to upset her by bringing up the subject."

I was impressed with Cheryl's consideration of her mother's feelings and that is why I agreed to assist her without her parents' consent.

I received several letters from Cheryl but did not have time to reply to all of them. Her letters were filled with unanswered questions about her birth, the strong bond she felt toward somebody and her years of growing up with adopted parents and an adopted sister. I realized after a while that Cheryl was venting some of her penned up anger in several of those letters to me.

She often wrote about her adopted mother. "My mother couldn't have any children of her own, therefore since society dictated that a woman was meant to have children in order to be a complete woman in the eyes of the world, mother simply went out and adopted two babies, whom she would always pretend she had given birth to. Her image was the most important thing in her life – her "stature in the community."

"I remember all of the teas she had at our house when we were growing up. My sister and I were expected to serve the tea and pass around all of the dainties. We were instructed never to speak unless spoken to. The women in the community would remark how nice mother's children were, and mother would feel accepted and respected. I hated serving at those teas, but most of all I resented the pretence that we were direct products of an affectionate, loving and perfect mother."

I asked Cheryl in a letter about her father, hoping that she may have been "daddy's little girl," and feel some warmth and love toward him. She replied to my question in her very next letter.

"I think Dad really wanted to adopt boys, because from the age of ten onward, my sister and I were expected to work in the fields with him stacking bales. When we were older we had to run the baler and stack the bales ourselves. We were also expected to carry big rocks from the field over to the fence lines. Never once did Dad ever thank us or reward us. It was just expected that we work in the field whenever he said so.

"It was Dad who forced me into taking piano lessons. My sister had to take violin lessons, which she hated. At least I was able to play the piano by ear. I had always been able to hear music on the radio and then sit down and play that same song on the piano. After Dad heard me a few times he insisted that I take piano lessons because he felt I had a natural talent. I was a concert pianist by the age of 18. I hated it when my Dad called me his little 'protégé', as though he had something to do with my talent."

In the letters that followed, Cheryl painted such a dark picture of her parents, who she said had tried to mould her into a carbon copy of themselves, never allowing her to express her own thoughts or satisfy her own needs. Well, she was certainly expressing them now.

The search for her birth mother was her own secret private expression, one she wasn't about to share with either of her parents. She told me that ever since she had started this search she had been having a lot of night-mares and dreams that had upset her. After that, she evidently joined a night class called "Dreams and Their Meanings" in the hope of analyzing what her dreams meant. I could relate to Cheryl's concerns, because as a child myself, I remembered that I too had terrorizing nightmares of someone or something chasing me. My Grandmother tried to console me, telling me that the tigers in my dreams would never catch me unless I ran away! I hadn't really understood what that meant. Was

I to stand there and be caught, or was I to run away? I wasn't sure.

Finally Cheryl's background information sheets arrived, along with her Adoption Order.

Her birth mother was said to have been 23 years of age at the time of Cheryl's birth in 1940. She was French, Protestant, and her height was 5'5". She had green eyes and red hair. She was "musically inclined." There was no other information given. There was no information whatsoever available on Cheryl's birth father. At the top of the document, the words "Birth Date" stated "September 5, 1940", "Date of Relinquishment – December 14, 1940." There was a three month span there that caused me to wonder where Cheryl had been during those three months. Had she been with her birth mother – or was she in a foster home or an orphanage waiting to be adopted?

Cheryl's Adoption Order read: "In the matter of a Petition for the Adoption of SHARLENE MARIE CANTIN." I glanced down the document but there were no clues as to her birth mother's name. The Order contained the names of her adoptive parents, the Superintendent of Child Welfare, sponsors of the adopting parents, and of course the words, "And it appearing that the consent of the parent or guardian of said child has been obtained."

Everything seemed to be in order except that there was not very much information on Cheryl's birth mother. Normally a birth mother's occupation appears, as well as her educational standing, and some information about the birth mother's parents, brothers and sisters and even their ages and occupations. There was also no mention of medical information. I questioned myself as to why there was no information on Cheryl's birth father. Had her birth mother hated him that much that she wouldn't even describe him to a social worker?

The letter that came along with the documents from the government stated, "We have no further information in our files." With that statement, there didn't seem much sense in writing back to the Government requesting additional information.

In the next two weeks I went through all of the Alberta telephone books and made a list of all of the Cantin families, which was 28 in all. I sent the list to Cheryl along with a letter format and asked that she send out letters to one-half of the Cantin families, while I sent out the other half. The letter simply stated that, "I believe that I have relatives here in Alberta by the name of Cantin of French origin, and I would love to find them." We were hoping that her birth mother would recognize the signature, "Sharlene Marie Cantin." It took about two months to send out all of the letters. I sent out my half as I could afford the price of the stamps and envelopes.

In the months following, many of the people who replied told all about their ancestry; when they arrived in Canada, the names and ages of their children, and some asked for more information, which we furnished in a second letter.

In the second letter we were a little more specific, describing Cheryl's birth mother as "a cousin who would have been born about 1917. There were a few replies from Cantin families who had no relatives in Canada. After six months we had heard from all but five families. I asked Cheryl to either telephone them herself, or if she wished me to, I would telephone them.

I asked Cheryl to please send me about $25.00 to cover the cost of the telephone calls. As a single mother of three children, I had very little funds available for assisting adoptees. I did not charge a fee for my services in any of the searches I was working on, but if I had to pay out money, I appreciated being reimbursed.

In Cheryl's reply she stated, "I have to work very hard to earn my money and hate to spend it this way, but if you feel it's really necessary, I am enclosing a money order for $20.00. How much longer do you think this search will take?"

When I read her letter I felt disillusioned and unappreciated. However, I contacted four of the five Cantin families during the next few days, only to find that none of them knew a lady both in 1917 whose maiden name had been Cantin, nor were they related to any Cantin families in Alberta.

There was only one family left and that was an "I. Cantin." I dialed the last number, hoping that this Cantin family would be the right one. The telephone rang and rang, and then a recording stated, "The phone number you have just dialled is out of service at this time. Please check your local listing, etc."

At that point I didn't know what to do next. Could it have been possible that we had already contacted the correct family, but I had not worded the letter specific enough? – or perhaps Cheryl's birth mother had read the letter but did not want to be found.

In the next month I continued to receive letters from

Cheryl, at least one a week. She sent me all of the replies she had received from the Cantin families she had written to. I went over and over the letters hoping to see something I hadn't noticed before. Somehow I felt that I had overlooked something. Some adoptees may have felt the same thing; that the answer they are seeking is already right there in their file, but they had not recognized it. I was beginning to think that Cheryl's birth mother was non-existent. It was like coming up against a brick wall – and yet, I knew she was out there somewhere – eating, sleeping, breathing and doing all of the normal daily things we all do like scrubbing floors, doing laundry and hanging clean clothes out on a clothes line. I held Cheryl's Adoption Order in my hands, reading and re-reading the words on the page, "And it appearing that the consent of the parent or guardian of said child has been obtained..."

It is sometimes a good idea to underline in yellow all of the vital words on an Adoption Order and background information so that those words will stand out. I tried to visualize Cheryl's birth mother sitting in front of a Social Worker in the Child Welfare Office some 40 years ago. She must have spoken to the social worker and the social worker must have asked her questions. Though scant, she must have given some information to be put on file. There must have been lots of questions she didn't answer. She must have signed the appropriate relinquishment documents. "She is real!" I would say to myself over and over again. "Her fingerprints must be on these documents – but who is she? Where is she?"

I totally frustrated myself each day reading through

the documents, the letters, history books on each of the towns in Alberta, sitting quietly – contemplating where she might be. The only one thing I could imagine was that Cheryl's birth mother's entire family had either died or moved to another province, otherwise why couldn't somebody lead us to her?

Finally I decided to phone "I. Cantin" once again. Much to my disappointment there was still a recording on her phone, but now the recording was one of disconnect. I contacted Directory Assistance and felt enlightened to find that I. Cantin had a new telephone number.

When everything was nice and quiet and I knew I would not be disturbed, I dialed the number. As it turned out it was an Irene Cantin. Unfortunately, there was nobody in her family born in 1917 whose maiden name had been Cantin. We talked a little about the French ancestry of the Cantin name. Then she said, "Way back about two generations ago – our real surname had been Cansineau. Somewhere along the line somebody short-ened and anglicized the name to Cantin."

After my conversation with I. Cantin, I now had brand new ideas – a brand new name to search for. I felt encouraged enough to remove at least one brick.

The next day I went to the library in a city two hours away and found out where the French commun-ities were in the province. I looked through telephone books in those communities and found in all – about six Cansineau families. I returned home with this new and exciting information.

The first thing I did was phone a girlfriend of mine – Emily, who lived in the same town as three of the

Cansineau families. I felt that she could tell me all about those three families. I gave Emily all of the information I had on Cheryl's birth mother. Emily had a copy of that town's history book and read the Cansineau family histories to me over the telephone. The Cansineau family had lived in this province prior to the First World War. The parents married about 1915 and had a little girl Marie, born in 1917, and five sons born between 1918 and 1925. It went on to describe the Flu Epidemic of 1918-19, the hungry 30's, the Second World War, and then it began listing who each of their children had married, where they live now, and it named their children. At that point I was not only interested in Marie born in 1917, I was also very interested in the sons born afterwards. If I was unable to locate Marie – perhaps one of her brothers would know her present whereabouts.

When I asked Emily to repeat the information on Marie's marriage, I was astonished when she said, "I know Marie quite well. She's back living in Canada. She and her husband spent the last thirty years living in Great Britain and South Africa where her husband worked. When he died she moved back here."

I asked my friend if Marie had any children, and she said "Yes, Marie has two sons who also live here." I asked her if Marie had ever used the name Cantin. She said she was sure that Marie and two of her sons had never changed their names to Cantin. The three brothers who had stayed on the farm had maintained the name Cansineau. "The two Cansineau brothers who had left – now live in another province." I thought to myself, "that would account for the fact that there were no Cantin families in the province who were related to Marie.

The next morning I telephoned Cheryl and told her all that had transpired.

"Are you sure it's her?" she questioned me.

"One can never be sure," I said. "But let's look at the facts.

- No other Cantin families had daughters born in 1917 – plus!.

- This Marie Cansineau was the right age – plus.

- She had used the name "Cantin" in her relinquishment documents – plus!

- Your middle name at birth was Marie – plus!

"These are all good signs that we could be on the right track."

I briefed Cheryl on what to say to Marie in a telephone call to her, and the time of day to telephone her. Cheryl was very anxious to make the telephone call as soon as possible. She said she would phone me back after she had spoken with Marie.

The very next morning my telephone rang and it was Cheryl.

"Hi!" she giggled. "It was her." She continued, "When I started talking to her she just listened to what I had to say about my search for my birth mother and my need to find her. Then I stopped talking because it almost seemed as though there was nobody on the other end of the phone. I couldn't even hear any breathing. Then all of a sudden I could hear her crying. After a minute or so, she quietly said, sobbing as she spoke, 'I can't believe this is really happening. Are you my little baby girl Sharlene?'

Then Cheryl said to me, "I told Marie my birth date, where I was born, and the name given to me at birth according to my Adoption Order. Again I could hear her sobbing. Since she seemed very upset, I told her that I could phone her back later. Then she said, "No!" as though in a panic that she would lose me again. She asked me for my name and telephone number, which I gave to her. She said she would phone me back in the afternoon."

I had prompted Cheryl earlier to always repeat any telephone numbers because people are sometimes nervous and shaking so much that they will reverse a number. Cheryl said that she had Marie repeat her telephone number more than twice. .

"I am so happy," Cheryl said. "You can't imagine how wonderful it was to hear her voice. Just to know that she is real and she is alive. I remember once in a dream I had. I heard a knock at the door. When I opened the door, a beautiful lady and handsome gentleman stepped forward. The lady said to me – 'I am your mother and this is your father.' Just as I was about to run into their arms, they raised their wings and flew away."

I laughed at Cheryl's dreams and could relate to them. I said, "Marie is not going to fly away. She will telephone you this afternoon – I'm sure of it! She just needs a little time to pull herself together. This has probably been quite a shock for her."

Cheryl said excitedly, "I can't wait to see what she

looks like - to see if I look like her. I never dreamt it would be this exciting."

(Was this the end of this beautiful story? No - not yet. I am shaking my head, uh uh.))

....

Later that evening Cheryl phoned me again to say that Marie had phoned her and that they had a long talk. Marie said that Cheryl's phone call was the answer to her prayers.

Cheryl told Marie all about my part in her search, and evidently Marie asked Cheryl if it would be possible for the two of them to come and visit me for a weekend. Cheryl said to me, "I am quite excited to meet you myself. I have only imagined what you look like." I admitted to Cheryl that I too had wondered what she looks like and that I would love to meet her birth mother as well.

The very next evening I received a phone call from Marie. She thanked me for assisting Cheryl in finding her. She told me how much it meant to her to finally know where Cheryl is. She asked if it would be okay if she and Cheryl came to visit me the next weekend. I, of course, agreed.

I spent the rest of the week cleaning my house and planning meals for the exciting weekend to come. About noon on Saturday I saw a car pull into my driveway. I was excited as I dashed to open the door. Both of them were smiling as they ran up the steps to my doorway. Cheryl grabbed me and hugged me. "This is my mother," she said, with a proud smile on her face. Marie threw her arms around me and I could feel her sobbing.

"Come on in you two. Make yourselves at home." I opened a bottle of champagne I had chilling, and poured three glasses. We toasted the beginning of a new and wonderful friendship.

Now, you would think that this is the end of a very wonderful true story, however, two things: first – this could be an Intermission – and secondly, there is a reason why this is called "Pandora's Box."

....

We talked and stared at one another all through lunch. It was easy to tell that Cheryl was Marie's daughter; just a younger version of herself. Cheryl had light blonde hair, Marie's hair was now dark blonde. They both had green eyes and slim figures. After lunch we sat out on the patio in the warm sun, listening to Marie talk about faraway places where she and her husband had lived.

I wasn't sure how much Marie had told Cheryl on their two hour drive to my house. As Marie began to talk about Cheryl's birth and the time they had spent together, I realized that they hadn't talked about that yet. I wondered at first if I was perhaps intruding by continuing to sit there listening; but then perhaps Marie wanted both of us to know the truth.

Marie looked at Cheryl and remarked, "I loved your father Paul very much. We had at one time talked about getting married. We were very much in love, but his family was wealthy and prominent, and my family was common and very poor. He did walk out on me, but I don't think he wanted to."

Then Cheryl interrupted, "You don't have to talk about this if it's too painful for you." I was glad that Cheryl was trying to put Marie at ease. But, Marie continued, "I want both of you to know the truth. I want everything out in the open."

"After you were born I waited for Paul to come and get both of us at the hospital, but he never did come. Regardless, there was no way that I was going to give you up for adoption. The nurses and social worker tried to get me to sign relinquishment papers but I wouldn't sign them. Instead – I persuaded the Matron at the Home for Unwed Mothers to give me a job and let us stay there for three months or so.

"I looked after you myself, nursing you every few hours, and when you slept I washed floors, prepared meals, made beds, and cleaned."

Cheryl and I looked at one another and smiled. This must be "the bond" that Cheryl had talked about so much. Medical authorities have often said that a baby will bond to a mother more quickly if the mother nurses her baby.

Marie continued.

"I didn't care what I had to do. At least we were together and we were safe. My little Sharlene was four months old when I made arrangements with one of my brothers and his wife to go and stay with them when we left the Home. They said they would take care of us until I could get on my feet. I had a good education and experience in accounting and secretarial work. I knew that we would make out okay.

"About the middle of December on a Thursday, I was getting ready for us to move to my brother's house the following Sunday. I woke up beside you and fed you that morning and when you went to sleep I got busy working at my morning chores. When breakfast was over and the dishes were done, I went to our room to check on you and continue packing. I opened the door to find that your crib was empty. I went all around the room in a panic, looking everywhere, but you were nowhere in the room. I ran down the hall and into the Matron's office without knocking.

"I was shouting over and over again – 'My baby is gone', 'My baby is gone.' I remember the matron grabbing my arms, telling me to calm down.

"I just kept shouting that my baby was gone."

As I listened to Marie sitting there on the deck, I looked over at Cheryl to see tears streaming down her cheeks. Marie was looking off in a distance, and I could tell that she was trying to remember the events as they had happened, and at the same time she was trying to hold back her tears.

I had to work hard to hold back my own tears. I took a deep breath, sighing loudly and said, "Why don't we talk about this later Marie?"

"No," Marie said emphatically. She looked at Cheryl

and said, "I have to tell you this now. You have to know the truth."

Marie looked at me and said,

"Ever since Cheryl's telephone call to me I have been thinking about what I should say to her. I have to tell both of you the truth about what happened. I have never been able to say this to anyone before, but I have to say it now."

It was obvious that Marie had kept all of this pain pent up inside of her all of these years, and at last she was able to get it all out. (Just like the title of this book, "The Tigers in your dreams will never catch you unless you run away.")

"Continue," I said.

"I remember the matron grabbing my arms and sitting me down in a chair in her office. I couldn't sit – I was in a panic to look for my baby. The matron kept hold of my arms down, keeping me from jumping up and running from her office. She told me to get hold of myself and she would explain where my baby was.

"I stopped crying and looked into her face – waiting.

She let go of my arms and sat up on the desk in front of me as though guarding me.

"Then she told me that a man and his wife had come to the Home asking to adopt a baby. They had told the matron that they could not have any children of their own. Evidently they pleaded with her. Then the matron told them that the only baby available was a little girl a couple of months old, whose mother was unmarried.

"At that point I screamed at the matron – No! No! – not Sharlene!

"She told me to calm down. She then said she felt it was in the best interest of my baby and me that Sharlene be placed with real parents – a mother and a father – who would give her a real home.

Marie continued, "I remember that day as though it was only yesterday. I screamed at the matron over and over again – 'You stole my baby! You stole my baby!'

"I remember running from the room, out the door of the Home and down the street. I didn't even pack my clothes. When I got to my brother's house, I was hysterical. My brother phoned a doctor. When he arrived, he gave me a sedative and suggested that I be hospitalized for a few days where he could keep an eye on me.

"I don't remember very much about the remainder of that day – but I do remember that it was December 13, 1940. I shall never forget that day. I woke up in the hospital the next morning. I could see nurses and doctors through the windows walking back and forth in the hallways. I laid there feeling numb. Then a doctor came in to talk to me. I started shouting, telling him what had happened, hoping that he could do something about it. He just patted my arm and then he left. A nurse came in and put a needle in my arm. I fell off to sleep again.

"When I got out of the hospital about three days later, I walked in a daze for hours and hours. I finally found my way to my brother's house. I don't remember much about the weeks that followed – other than feeling numb.

"Years later I met a wonderful man. After we became friends, I told him what had happened to me. He held me in his arms as I cried. A few months after that, he and I were married. Then we were transferred to England. We were worlds away from my past – worlds away from the pain that had once hurt me so deeply. We then moved to South Africa. After my husband died last year, I came back to Canada."

Marie told us that even though she and her husband have two wonderful sons, she has never ever forgotten about her little baby Sharleen.

At that point Marie broke down and cried as though relieved to get her painful past finally out in the open. Cheryl pulled her chair close to Marie and rubbed her back. I was stunned at the thought of what Marie had gone through – here in Canada; right here in Alberta. I got up and went into the house to put on some coffee. (But what I was really thinking was, "I need a drink!"

I glanced toward the patio and could see Marie and Cheryl crying in one another's arms. They needed time alone, which I gave to them.

Later on and after coffee time, we enjoyed "Happy Hour" followed by a candle lit dinner. That evening we looked at photographs that each of them had brought along. They reminisced through the entire evening until we were all exhausted.

After a good night's sleep, the next day was wonderful. We had breakfast on the patio and then went for a drive. We stopped for lunch at an expensive restaurant, walking in separately and pretending we were tourists who recognized one another across the room.

Late that afternoon Cheryl and Marie left. I felt so alone when they drove away, but I was pleased to know how completely happy they both were. All of the work and the frustration was worth Cheryl's $20.00 – just seeing them together at long last. I remembered the bond that Cheryl had felt. The feeling that she had while growing up that she had felt affection from somebody. I was sure that in the months to follow, Cheryl would have all of her questions answered.

(This would be a wonderful ending to this story, however, the title "Pandora's Box" is still coming.)

....

The next morning I telephoned Social Services. I was careful how I worded my request, deliberately putting Marie in the negative in order to get the information I wanted. I told the social worker all about Marie and Cheryl meeting one another, and stated, "Marie says she can't remember signing any type of relinquishment document. Of course that can't be true."

I asked, "Can you check the file and see if you can find anything with Marie's signature on it so that I can tell her the name of the document she had signed? She would be very relieved to have this information." The Social Worker asked me to phone him back that afternoon.

When I phoned back, he said, "I checked through

every document in the file, and there is absolutely nothing signed by this Marie relinquishing her baby for adoption."

I sat down by the phone after I had hung up, thinking about the torment this poor woman had been put through because of one person – a Matron at a Home for Unwed Mothers that took it upon herself to play God." I shook my head as I realized how, in this world, one person can so drastically affect and change the lives of so many people.

Marie had not sat in front of a social worker answering questions. Neither her signature nor her fingerprints were on any document as I had earlier speculated. When I remembered the words "And it appearing that the consent of the parent or guardian of said child has been obtained…"

I now knew that this was not true, but how had the Matron gotten around this? How did Social Services allow a child to be adopted without the mother's consent and without her written signature? The matron at the home knew very little about Marie, and knew nothing of Sharlene's father, which would account for the fact that there was no information on file about Cheryl's father.

I wondered why the Superintendent of Social Services had permitted the adoption. The matron at the Home must have lied when she presented an extremely negative and believable story in order for the Superintendent to approve the adoption without the mother's consent.

About two weeks later, Cheryl telephoned me. She told me that she was thrilled to have met her two half brothers. Marie had been a little worried about their reaction at first because sons do have a tendency to place their mothers high upon a pedestal. Cheryl said they were pleased to hear that they have a sister, and couldn't wait to meet her. Cheryl told me that the day she met her two brothers, they presented her with 40 long-stemmed red roses, which they said was "one rose for every year we have been apart."

About four months later, Cheryl telephoned me to say that Marie was very happy to provide her with her father's name. She asked me, "do you think you could find him?"

It took about two hours to find her birth father Paul. I could see his name listed in the telephone book for Victoria. When I phoned Cheryl, her immediate response was, "I want to go and meet him. Will you come with me?"

Then I asked Cheryl, "How does Marie feel about you going to see your birth father?"

Cheryl replied, "I think she's more excited about it than I am. She told me all about him and about how much they had been in love. "I think she may still love him."

I couldn't help but wonder at this point, with Marie being a widow, if she hoped that perhaps she and Paul could start where they had left off. For that to happen, Paul would have to either be single, or a widower.

A couple of weeks later Cheryl and I boarded a plane to Victoria. We checked into a hotel downtown. The next day we set out to the district where Paul lives. We found his house and walked past it a couple of times hoping to get a glimpse of Paul outside mowing the lawn or washing his car. We couldn't see anybody, but there was a car in the driveway. We went to a restaurant close by and ordered coffee. As agreed, I went over to the telephone, looked up Paul's telephone number, and dialled. Cheryl could not see or hear me from where she was sitting which was the way I wanted it.

The telephone rang. Then a lady answered.

I asked, "Could I speak to Paul please?"

"Who's speaking," she responded in a demanding tone.

I told her that I was an old school friend from many years ago just visiting in Victoria. She then said more calmly, "Paul died six months ago." I then said, "I'm so sorry" and before she could ask me any more questions, I hung up.

As I approached Cheryl I wished that I had been anywhere but there.

I sat down and stirred my coffee.

"Well?" Cheryl asked. "Did you speak to him?" I continued stirring my coffee.

"What?" Cheryl questioned. "Tell me! What did he say?"

I looked up at Cheryl and said quietly, "I'm so sorry Cheryl to have to tell you this, but your father died only six months ago."

Cheryl looked heart broken. Her hopes were gone with just one phone call, one sentence. I could see that she had tears in her eyes.

"Let's go," I said. We left the restaurant and went back to our hotel. Cheryl sat on the bed, with her back to me, looking out the window. This was a situation that nothing and nobody could rectify. Then I contemplated what could be the next best thing. I dismissed the idea of telephoning Paul's wife back. She probably would never want to know that he had a daughter out there somewhere. She may not have even known about Marie.

Paul's last name was very uncommon. I looked in the telephone book to see if there was anyone listed with the same surname – there was one. Cheryl was still looking out the window – not paying any attention to me. I sat down on my bed, picked up the telephone and dialled.

When a man answered I asked him if he could possibly be Paul's brother. Cheryl turned around abruptly and stared at me.

The man replied, "Yes, I am his brother." I proceeded to tell him exactly who I was, who Cheryl was, and why we were in Victoria. I added that – I knew that Paul was now deceased.

The man didn't seem shocked at all. I asked him about Paul, and he began telling me all about him.

I interrupted him, saying "Could I possibly put your niece Cheryl on the telephone, and could you tell her all about her father?" The man replied in a tone that led me to believe that he had known about Cheryl. "Of course," he replied, "I would love to talk to her."

Cheryl smiled at me and took the telephone. I handed her a pen and paper so that she could make notes. As they spoke to one another I could see Cheryl jotting down all kinds of information about Paul. He had been in the Air Force, received a medal for bravery. She wrote down the names of countries, probably where he had been stationed during the war. Then I saw her jot down a woman's name and some other names.

Cheryl asked if it would be possible for them to write to one another, and I could see from her facial expression that she was pleased with his reply. When Cheryl hung up, she said to me:

"He said we could write to one another. He has lots of pictures of my father that he said he would send to me. My father married a woman by the name of Henrietta and they have two children. He suggested that I not contact any of them because he did not think that they would be receptive."

After returning home, I assumed that Cheryl would tell Marie all about our trip and our findings. In a few weeks I received a lovely letter from Cheryl telling me that she had received a letter from her Uncle and that he had also sent two photo albums filled with pictures and newspaper articles about her father.

"Some of the photographs are 5"x7" and some are 8"x10", all suitable for framing."

One morning about a month later, I received a letter with Marie's name and return address at the top of the envelope. I slit it open to find that inside – was a letter addressed to Cheryl. At first I thought she must have written to both of us at the same time and mixed up the two letters. Then at the bottom of the letter there was a notation that this letter was merely a carbon copy of a letter she sent to Cheryl. The letter began

Cheryl.

How could you possibly say such an awful thing to

me. Accusing me like that is unforgivable. Paul is your father whether you want to believe it or not. I never dreamed you would turn on me like this. I would never have believed you could be so cruel and insensitive. The letter was simply signed "Marie."

I immediately telephoned Cheryl to find out what in the "H" was going on. I told her about the letter I had received. She mumbled "I got one too!" Then I asked her, "What did you say to Marie? What is this all about?"

Cheryl replied, "I received a letter from my Uncle a couple of weeks ago. He said in his letter, 'My brother denied being the father of that child'."

Cheryl went on to explain to me, "I was so upset when I received my Uncle's letter that I wrote to Marie immediately and told her what my Uncle had said. My Uncle told me that my father denied being the father of that child."

"Because of what my Uncle said, I demanded that Marie tell me who else she was sleeping with at the time."

"Cheryl!" I shouted into the receiver. "You didn't actually say that to her?"

"Yes I did!" she shouted. "Imagine her lying to me like that, telling me that Paul was my father when he wasn't. I have a right to know who my father is! He's probably still alive somewhere. I have a right to know who he is."

There was a long pause – and then I said to her, "But you know Paul was your father." There was another long pause, and then I added "Tell me Cheryl – if your Uncle didn't believe you were his brother's daughter, then why would he send you all of those albums of photographs and newspaper clippings about his brother? – Think about it."

"I don't know," she replied. "Maybe he didn't know! – I don't know!"

"Oh! for Heaven sakes Cheryl. Marie told you openly that Paul was your father. How could you not believe her? Another thing – how could you possibly question Marie's fidelity after all that she had been through. She loved Paul and he loved her. She fought to keep you. How can you turn on her like this?"

Cheryl said calmly, "I didn't know what else to do when I received my Uncle's letter. I guess, without thinking, I immediately and spontaneously wrote to Marie demanding that she tell me the truth."

"Why didn't you phone me first – before you wrote to Marie?"

"I don't know. I guess I was so mad at what my Uncle had said that I acted impulsively."

I was thinking to myself, "Cheryl calls him her Uncle, she called Paul her father, and yet refers to herself as that child!"

"What should I do now?" Cheryl asked.

"What you do Cheryl is write a letter to Marie or better yet telephone her and beg her forgiveness."

The next morning I received a copy of a letter addressed to Cheryl from Marie's son. He said,

How dare you upset our mother. What right have you to call her down. She did everything to keep you when you were born. How ungrateful can you be? My brother and

I are sorry that you ever found us and better yet, we are sorry that you were ever born. Our mother is the finest person we know and we resent your insinuations. We're glad that somebody had the sense to give you away so that we didn't have to grow up with the likes of you. Don't ever write or telephone our mother ever again.

In the next few days I was not sure that Cheryl had written a letter of apology to Marie or not. Then I received another letter from Marie addressed to Cheryl. The letter read:

Cheryl:

You think that you can send a one sentence note saying you're sorry for what you said and that I would forgive you?

When I received your unconvincing apology, I was so mad that I phoned your Uncle in Victoria and we talked about the incident around Paul's supposed denial that he was your father. I now remember it very well.

The day I found out that I was pregnant, I went to see Paul at his house. I was scared and feeling very much alone. I told him that I was expecting his baby. He was happy and excited. We were talking quietly in the living room. We had already planned on getting married some day anyway, but when I told him I was going to have his baby, he insisted that we get married right away.

We talked about our wedding and our baby, not realizing that his mother and his brother were standing around the corner of the living room – listening to every word we said.

Then Paul's mother came into the living room and

started shouting, "You're not marrying that woman! She's not even in our class." Paul's mother demanded – "Paul, you deny being the father of that child."

Marie's letter continued, saying, "So you see Cheryl – it was not Paul who denied being the father of my child, it was his mother. She did not want me to tarnish their family's reputation nor to force Paul into having to pay child support. Marie said that she tried and tried to get Paul to stand up to his mother, but he just stood there and said nothing."

Perhaps wanting to get even with Cheryl, Marie threatened –

"I wonder how your adopted parents would feel if they knew what you have done to me. You have protected them from being hurt by not telling them about finding me, but you don't seem to care how you have hurt me. I have a good mind to write to them and tell them what kind of daughter they raised." The letter was signed, "Marie."

Cheryl telephoned me later that week to apologize to me for the way Marie was involving me in their problems. I said to her without any sympathy, "It's you who created this horrible mess!"

Cheryl said defensively, "But she didn't need to respond so maliciously."

"Listen to me Cheryl," I said. "If I bluntly accused you of infidelity you would scream at me, and you'd probably never speak to me again. At least Marie is still talking to you, even if it's at the top of her lungs."

There was a long pause. Then Cheryl said in a demanding voice as though I were to blame and as though I were the healer of all of Mankind, "Well, what do you suggest I do now?"

"I don't know what to suggest. Maybe in time all of the wounds will heal."

Cheryl then said defensively, "Do you see in her letter where she has the gaol to threaten to tell my parents all about my search for her?"

There was a long pause in our conversation, and then Cheryl confirmed, "I have wonderful parents. I'm glad they came to the Home that morning and took me away from that wretched woman. I'm glad I was adopted."

Eight years went by before I saw Cheryl again. In all of those years she had never communicated again with Marie and resents even the slightest mention of her. Cheryl is still corresponding with her Uncle now and then, the brother of the man who supposedly declared that he was "not the father of that child." Now I would love to ask Cheryl, "So – who was that child?"

Author's Note: I have often wondered what Paul would have thought of all of this if he had been watching from Heaven. I am hoping that Paul is forgiving Marie and that Marie has long since forgiven Cheryl. I believe that because I want to believe it!

Since this experience, I have reunited well over 400 adoptees with their biological families, however, I have never assisted any adoptee without the full consent and support of his or her adoptive parents.

In the introduction of this book I said that I had written it for two reasons. Both reasons hold true because I do want to show you and warn you what not to say and what not to do and why, and as for entertaining my readers, I want each one of you to cry a little when you pretend to open the lid and look inside of Pandora's box.

CHAPTER SEVEN

THE BALLERINA IN
THE MUSIC BOX

As a young child, Katy cried herself to sleep almost every night, hoping and praying that her birth mother would come and rescue her from the torture and torment she was going through at the hands of her adoptive mother Ethel. Ethel made sure that the black and blue marks on Katy's back, her legs and arms, were always covered up with coveralls and long sleeves, even during the heat of the summer months.

Her mother often threw slop pails at her. If in the morning Katy did not dump her mother's commode on time, that too was thrown into Katy's face. Those incidences were not as bad as the frequent occasions when her mother came at her with a pitchfork, leaving marks on her arms when Katy shielded her face from being cut open. Ethel repeatedly threatened Katy that if she ever told anyone about her black and blue marks, she would go to jail where she would be beaten daily and would have to survive without food.

As a very young child, Katy believed that every child went through the same treatment that she did. It was not until she went to school and saw how other children were being treated by their parents that Katy realized that the torture she was going through was only in her own home. Also, it was at that point that Katy resigned herself to the fact that her birth mother was never coming back.

Katy's adoptive father was a wonderful man. However, on the numerous occasions when he stuck up for Katy or tried to rescue her, he too was beaten with whatever object Ethel could lay her hands on.

There were never any gifts for Katy on birthdays or on Christmas morning, nor ever any recognition of any special occasions throughout the year.

Katy recalls the one day her father came home all smiles and excited. He handed Katy a brown paper bag with something inside. "For me?" Katy exclaimed, with giggling excitement. She opened up the bag, and inside it – was a little white jewelry box. Katy opened the lid and watched in amazement as a little ballerina danced around and around to music playing. Just then, her mother appeared, grabbed the jewelry box, threw it on the floor and stomped on it – smashing it into several pieces. Her mother glared at her father warning him never to buy anything like that ever again. Katy stared at the broken jewelry box, which was as broken as her own heart was.

Sandra Butler Ladwig

Katy was afraid to cry, because if she did, her mother would yell at her, "You stop crying or I will give you something to cry about!" Katy went to her room quietly – trying to hold back the tears until she could bury her face into her pillow.

Katy and her father endured years and years of physical and mental torture and abuse. One day her father packed his bags and moved to B.C., inviting Katy to come along with him. Since Ethel was quite ill at the time, Katy felt obliged to stay with her, trying to nurse her back to health. Bedridden and totally reliant on Katy, Ethel became quite human. One day she suggested, "After I'm gone, you really should find your own mother. I am sure that she loved you very much. I know she would like to see you." A few months later, Ethel died.

Katy managed to get a job at a bank in a nearby town, still living at home on her father's farm. It was about that time that she contracted Crones Disease, and a few years later, heart problems. In the years that followed, she married and had two sons. As a gift to Katy her father gave her the farmland and the farm buildings. Katy and her husband built a new home on the corner of one parcel, however it was never a happy home.

Following a lengthy separation and divorce, the judge awarded one half of the farm to Katy's husband. Now, mortgaged to the hilt, Katy tried her best to raise her two sons alone, and at the same time, hold onto the family farm that would some day be theirs. In the years that followed, Katy and her ex-husband did become friends of a sort. However, raising two sons alone and looking after cattle, horses, donkeys and farmland, there was no longer any time for thoughts of Katy's desire to some day find her birth mother.

About 1974, when Katy was in Calgary on bank business, she was in a restaurant at noon having lunch -when a young trucker came in and sat at the table next to her. Katy listened as he ordered a whopping big lunch, starting with Tomato Soup. He summoned the waitress over, asking for ketchup for his Tomato Soup. The waitress started teasing him, which made Katy laugh. Thinking two women were picking on him, the trucker began joking and then chatting with Katy. He introduced himself simply as "Alan." He seemed quite taken with Katy, a beautiful girl with long brown hair and large brown eyes. Katy and Alan spent the better part of two hours together, talking and sharing stories before Alan had to be on his way. A few days later when Alan returned to Calgary, he phoned Katy. During the next few months, they managed to go out on several dates. Caught up in a fairytale romance, Katy and Alan fell in love. They both felt such a strong bond to one another, especially since both of them were adopted and both had experienced failed marriages. They often talked about the importance of the two of them being best friends before any consideration of a marriage between them. One problem however, stood in their way. Alan was still married, although going through what he called an "atrocious divorce." Unfortunately, as a result of continuous financial demands on Alan by his estranged wife, and a trucking job that took him from coast to coast, he and Katy regrettably drifted apart.

Katy continued on as a single mother raising two

wonderful sons, working at the bank and farming evenings and weekends.

One day in 1985, a neighbor of Katy's rushed into the bank and told Katy that she had heard on the news that adoptees could send a letter to the government requesting information about their biological mothers and fathers. Katy wasted no time in writing a letter to the government requesting information about her birth and subsequent adoption.

Four months later a letter arrived. Her hands were shaking as she opened it. Her Adoption Order said that her birth name was Louise Marie Anderson, born in a coal-mining town. Background information enclosed showed that her Mother had been 31 years old in 1946 when Katy was born, single, born in Saskatchewan, Dutch, protestant, and a homemaker. It stated that her mother was 5'-3" in height, 114 lbs.. medium complexion, blue eyes and brown hair. Her mother had one brother and three sisters. The information listed Katy's birth father as 30 years of age, single, Irish, and a factory worker.

Also enclosed were forms Katy could fill out and return to the government that would register her in their Post Adoption Registry. That meant that if her birth mother, birth father or any siblings also registered, the Government would reunite them. Katy filled out the forms that very night and sent them back to the Government. Weeks went by, months and then years with no notification from the Government that anyone in her birth family had registered looking for her.

In 1991 Katy heard about an organization in Calgary

called "TRIAD" that assists adoptees in finding their birth parents. She wrote a letter to them requesting their assistance and sent along all of the information she had received from the government about her birth mother and birth father.

Just a few days later, Katy received a telephone call from a lady who said she was from TRIAD, and was pleased to report that they had her brother registered with them. Katy was very excited and amazed to learn that she had a brother. After arrangements were made to meet her brother, Katy sat in wonderment about what he would look like and she was also hopeful that her brother might know the whereabouts of their Mother and Father.

The next afternoon Katy drove to Calgary to meet her brother in the TRIAD office. That day was one of the happiest days in her life. She walked into the TRIAD office and was ushered into an empty room. Soon she heard voices and the door open. She stood up so that she would be face to face with her brother as he walked through the door. The girl from TRIAD stood aside as Katy looked into the face of her brother for the first time.

All of a sudden both of them gasped. There, standing before her was Alan. They stared and stared at one another in absolute shock.

Later that day, as Katy and Alan dined together, they talked about what would have happened had they married back in 1974, and worse yet, what if they had had children? Unfortunately Alan knew nothing about his birth mother or birth father.

Katy asked Alan why he had not registered in the

government's Post Adoption Registry. He replied, "I did register in 1986!" Katy was furious to think that she could have met her brother five years before. When Katy got home that evening, she wrote a letter to the Post Adoption Registry indicating that she had registered in 1985 and her brother Alan had registered in 1986 – asking why were they not reunited five years before? The reply to her letter stated, "We apologize that you and your brother were not reunited five years ago. We seem to have lost the files!" That was their only comment and excuse!

Later that year Katy became quite ill, hospitalized first in a small town hospital, and then transferred by ambulance to Edmonton. One day she heard the specialists talking outside of her door, one saying to the other, "It's only a matter of time before she dies!" One doctor then told her that she should contact her family and get her affairs in order." She watched as her one leg became darker and darker and then turned black. Her doctor told her that if the new medication they were trying on her did not work, it was likely that she would lose her leg. Fortunately her leg began getting better. Soon it returned to its natural color. In only a few months Katy was able to return home to the farm, however, she was no longer strong enough to work on the farm or at the bank. Alan decided to quit his job as a trucker and move to Katy's farm and run it for her. That decision was a Godsend for Katy and her boys.

During the next two years, Katy's health improved to the point where she could help Alan with the chores, the cattle and the crops. They began to raise horses and donkeys, naming each one.

One evening while discussing the possibility of locating their birth mother and birth father, Alan brought out his adoption papers. He too was born in the same coal-mining town where Katy was born. The background information stated that his birth mother was 29 years of age in 1944, married, born in Saskatchewan, Dutch, protestant, with a Grade 8 education, working as a housewife. Her height also was 5'-3", weight 112 lbs., with blue eyes, brown hair and medium complexion. It also stated that her parents were both living at the time of Alan's birth. His documents stated that his grandfather was 60 years old, working in shipyards, and his grandmother was age 58 and was a housewife.

Both Katy and Alan could not imagine where those shipyards could have been. They were definitely not here anywhere on the prairies. Perhaps they were in Vancouver or Victoria. Alan's documents stated that his birth mother had one brother age 17 who was a student and three sisters ages 24, 19 and 14. The oldest sister was in the military reserve (navy) and the other two were students. The government's records indicated that Alan was the third child born to his birth mother.

On weekends Katy and Alan traveled short distances to mining towns, trying to find out about their birth family. Numerous inquiries in person and phone calls turned up nothing. It was as though their mother and father had never existed. One major problem was that, – during the Second World War, thousands of men went to work in coal mines. Once the war was over, they all scattered across the province or back home to other provinces. Those who remained in the coal-mine towns had been homesteaders – long since now deceased.

....

It was about this time that I had the pleasure of meeting Katy and Alan. They each provided me with their adoption documents and background information.

It took me a year and a half to track down every Anderson family that had lived in the small mining town where Katy and Alan had been born.

I contacted the hospital where they were both supposedly born. However, the Director of Medical Records would not provide confirmation of their births nor any information about their Mother. I then contacted the Administrator of the Hospital, who asked for my phone number stating that he would phone me after the office was closed. At the time, I thought that that was a strange request, but I was not about to question why.

That evening the Administrator phoned me and he confirmed that Alan was born on September 1, 1944. However, he could not find any record of Katy's birth. He did say that there had been another hospital in a small mining town nearby that was now a bar. The Administrator was pleased to tell me that Alan's birth mother was listed as Marie Anderson. When I phoned Katy and Alan and told them what their mother's name was, both of them were naturally delighted. In trying to search out medical records from the other hospital, a longtime resident told me that when the War was over, a pit was dug and all of the medical records from that hospital were buried, primarily to cover up evidence of what the wives at home were up to while their husbands were overseas.

I placed an ad in the local newspaper of the town where Alan was born, asking if anyone could remember Marie Anderson. Those who replied could not remember her, but promised to make inquiries. I spoke with a retired doctor who had worked in the hospital back in the 1940's. He said it was difficult for him to remember back 53 years ago, especially when there were thousands of people living in that mining town during and after the war.

Katy's adoptive father John, was now living in a nursing home close to his farm. One morning, bright and early, Katy and I went to see John, hoping that his memory would be clearer and sharper in the morning. After the usual introductions and small talk, I started asking John questions about when he and Ethel went to Calgary to get Katy. He said that they went to a large building much like a factory. He said that in one large room there were babies in cribs all around him. The babies were sectioned off according to racial origin and religion. John and Ethel were ushered to one section where there were about six babies they could choose from.

John said that Katy was so beautiful, and a little older than the other babies. His heart immediately went out to her especially when she reached out and touched his hand. John said that he was not interested in looking at any of the other five babies. He recalled that he went back to Calgary and managed to persuade one of the Social Workers into telling him who Katy's biological parents were. He then said that he set out to the coal-mining town where Katy's biological mother lived.

I prodded Katy's Dad for more and more information about where he went to in that mining town. He could not remember if he had driven to a farmhouse or to a house in town. However, he did say that when he drove into the yard, a man and woman came out to greet him. When he had told them who he was, they invited him into their house. He could not remember if there were any other children milling about. He also could not remember the name of the woman or the man.

I asked John questions over and over and in different ways, but that was the only information I learned from John that day. Although I believed what he recalled to be true, I still could not feel the existence of a Marie Anderson.

Having contacted everyone by the name of Anderson and all of the old-timers in the area, my next step was to contact the local library in that small town. I asked the librarian to look up the old newspapers on microfilm and give me the names of mothers who had had babies at the same time that Alan was born. She provided me with four names. I was able to find only one mother still living. Luckily she was Marie Anderson's roommate.

The roommate recalled that the only reason she could remember Marie was because she was giving her baby boy up for adoption and she was crying a lot during those 10 days in hospital. She revealed that the new mother wanted so desperately to see her son, but the nurses wouldn't allow it. She also remembered that Marie's mother came to visit her in the hospital every day. She told me that Marie's mother was quite a large woman and therefore it was difficult for her to climb the long staircase to the second floor. Once she reached the chair beside her daughter's bed, she was always out of breath. Those words and messages were music to our ears, because it finally brought Marie Anderson to life for all three of us.

During the next few weeks, I contacted every Marie Anderson I could find in Saskatchewan, Alberta and British Columbia, to no avail.

Then one day I made another trip to the Provincial Archives. I had been there several times before, searching through various old records so I knew what records were held there. As I was flipping tediously through birth records for all of the cities and towns in Alberta, all of a sudden I noticed there were birth registers on file from the mining town where Alan was born. I ordered those birth registers to be brought to my table. When they arrived, I sat down and started going through them. I finally came to an entry for "Anderson, Alan, born September 1, 1944, mother Marie Magour (signed as Marie Anderson)." I could not believe my eyes. Blood rushed to my head. My heart was pounding. I was afraid I was just dreaming. I sat staring at the entry as one stares at a treasure map. I kept looking over my shoulder, first to the right and then the left, hoping that nobody had noticed the treasure chest I had found. I wrote down the entire entry just as it was written. I then left the Archives and drove home. I did not want to tell Katy and Alan what I had found until I had more concrete information.

In the next few days I searched everywhere for the

name "Magour," however, could not find even one in Canada. Then I went onto the Internet, and was fortunate, although skeptical, to find one listing in Arizona – a "Maxine Magour." I sent an E-mail message to Maxine Magour that evening, telling her all about Katy and Alan and their search for their mother Marie Magour. The next evening I was overjoyed, thrilled and elated to read:

> Yes, these are my relatives who once lived in Canada. I have one Aunt June who was in the military here in Seattle. Unfortunately she died only a few years ago. I also have an Uncle Walter who still lives in Seattle.
>
> I have one Aunt born in Alberta who remained in Alberta. Her name was Marie. Unfortunately Marie died of cancer in 1959. She married a George Anderson. I believe they had three children who are still living in Alberta.
>
> George remarried years later. I have lost contact with him. I do remember that my Aunts' father worked in the shipyards in Seattle.

That evening I contacted Uncle Walter in Seattle, and he told me that Marie's family still live in Alberta. He gave me the names: "Alben Anderson, Frank Anderson and Jane Anderson." He did not know Jane's married name.

That evening I was able to find a listing in the Calgary telephone directory for an Alben Anderson. The very next morning, I dialed his telephone number. A lady answered the telephone. I asked to speak to Alben. She told me she was his wife, and explained that he was out of town and would not return home until the next day. I then asked her for Jane's phone number, simply explaining that a relative was trying to contact her. Alben's wife said that if I would leave my name and phone number with her, she would ask Jane to phone me.

About two hours later Jane phoned me and I was very excited. I told her all about Katy. I was surprised to hear her say, "I knew I had a sister somewhere, but since she had been adopted out, I didn't want to intrude in her life by searching for her."

Then I told Jane all about Alan. Her reply was, "I have always suspected that I had a brother who was also given up for adoption." She told me a little about herself, her brother Alben, and her brother Frank, who all lived in Calgary.

I asked if they could come to our city to meet Katy and Alan the following weekend. She agreed that she and Frank could come, however, Alben had to work on weekends. Since I did not feel it was fair to exclude Alben, I asked if I could bring Katy and Alan to Calgary the next day. She agreed and said that she would arrange it with her two brothers. I told her that I was going to phone Katy and Alan right away and invite them over to my house. Being the romantic that I was, I asked, "Would you like to listen in on the telephone while I tell them about you, Alben and Frank?" She said she would be thrilled to listen in.

After I hung up, I phoned Katy and Alan and asked if they could come over. They arrived fairly late, saying that they could only stay a few minutes because they had to get home to feed the cattle and horses. I dialed Jane's phone number and when she answered, I told her to hold on. I sat the phone down close to me.

As I began to tell Katy and Alan all about finding the name Magour, my e-mail discussion with Maxine Magour, their Uncle Walter in Seattle and their sister Jane in Calgary, both Katy and Alan began to cry. I then added that unfortunately, their mother Marion had died in 1959. Katy buried her face in her hands and cried the tears of a little girl who had anticipated her mother coming back for her some day. There were tears rolling down Alan's face as well. This had been a very emotional and frustrating search. The three of us then had one big bear hug.

Then I remembered the telephone. I pointed, "Your sister is right there on the telephone listening to our conversation." Katy stared at the telephone receiver which was lying down next to her. She picked up the telephone, and between tears and laughter, Katy managed to have a conversation with Jane. She then handed the telephone to Alan, who held his composure throughout their lengthy conversation. Two hours later, Katy and Alan left.

The next day we drove to Calgary and followed Jane's directions to a shopping center. As soon as we parked our van, a car pulled up beside us. Alan and I got out of the van and approached them.

I walked toward a lady with the question "Jane?" She replied "yes!" I hugged her. Alan and Alben first shook hands and then they hugged one another. I turned around and Katy was nowhere to be seen. I went back to the van, opened the door, and there she was, looking frightened as though she had something to hide. I took her hand

and helped her out of the van. As she approached Jane, I could feel her hands shaking so I grabbed her arm. Jane reached out to Katy, and the two of them hugged and shed possibly 53 years of tears.

After the hugs and tears were over, we followed Jane and Alben to Jane's house. Once inside, we met Katy and Alan's brother Frank. His face showed the excitement of a little boy on Christmas morning. Once everybody was introduced to one another and seated in the living room, Jane proceeded to tell Katy and Alan all about their mother Marie. Jane had albums of photographs piled high on the coffee table.

The first photo shown to Katy was that of their mother Marie; the mother that she had prayed and cried about all of these years. I sat close and took a photograph of Katy looking down at her mother's face for the first time. I could see tears rolling down her cheeks as she intently studied her mother's face.

About 20 minutes later, Jane announced that the coffee was ready, and asked if everyone wanted to go to the kitchen. As these brothers and sisters all stood up, I seized the moment by asking if they would stand together for a photograph. Right after the flash went off, Frank commented, "That should be interesting! I imagine Mother will show herself somehow in that photograph!" I didn't pay too much attention to that comment at the time. I proceeded to take about twenty more photographs throughout the evening.

At the kitchen table, albums of old photographs of relatives were passed around, with explanations as to who they each were. After three hours of chatting and sharing years of their childhoods, Katy, Alan and I left for home.

Two weeks later, Frank, Jane and her husband arrived to spend the entire weekend with all of us at our lake cottage. Unfortunately, Alben was unable to come. My husband and I were the chief cook and bottle washers as the four Andersons got to know one another a little better.

After dinner, I was pleased to pass around the photographs I had taken two weeks prior in Calgary. I apologized that my camera must not have been working well that evening. There was a white smear across the side of the photograph of Katy looking at her mother's face for the first time, and also a white smear across the bottom of the photograph of the five Anderson children together for the first time. Frank looked closely at those two photographs, and then shouted, "What did I tell you? Mother was there!" I stared at those two photographs – not believing that it could be true.

A few days later, I took those two photographs to a professional photographer I knew. I explained to him, "I have never had this happen ever before. This is a very expensive camera and I used good film." The photographer studied the two prints and several others I handed to him, and then stated, "In all my years as a photographer, I have never seen anything like this before – it is truly bizarre." He then asked to see the negatives. He added, "On the negatives, if the white smear goes down below the bottom line of the photograph – it could be the film or your camera, however, if it doesn't, it is most unusual." Studying the negatives, it was clear that the white smear did not go beyond the side nor below the bottom line of the negative. As a matter of fact, there was no smear anywhere in or on the two negatives.

Katy and Alan talked a lot about their birth family that year. They kept asking questions and wondering about other family members. They were interested in meeting their Uncle Walter who still lived in Seattle.

That summer Katy and Alan turned the cattle and horses out to graze in the lush green fields and took the opportunity to go to Seattle to visit their Uncle Walter. Fortunately they had been able to become well acquainted and familiar with Uncle Walter through telephone calls and letters that included several photographs. I have always believed that "familiarity" is the most important word aside from "love."

In one of their conversations one evening, Uncle Walter said, "I don't know if this is important to you or not at this point in your lives, but I do believe that you have a right to know the truth. He looked at both Katy and Alan and then announced, "Marie is not your Mother, your real mother was June." Uncle Walter went on to explain "June was in the Navy here in the U.S. When she got pregnant she was very afraid that she would be discharged. Therefore, she faked an illness in each of your cases and got away with it."

Katy and Alan stared at Uncle Walter in disbelief. He shrugged his shoulders and he then said, "**It is what it is!**" Realizing that he was in deep enough trouble that he had some further explaining to do, Uncle Walter said, "I can't remember which of you was June's severe tonsillitis and which of you was June's perforated or ruptured appendix. Those were the reasons written in June's navy file. The reasons at the hospital were of course the truth."

Uncle Walter went on to say that he had no idea where Katy had been born. Perhaps they were both born at the same hospital and June lied about her name in both of the medical records.

Uncle Walter went on to say that it all came out in the wash and ended up to be a wonderful gift to two loving couples who desperately wanted to adopt a baby of their own that they could love and cherish for a lifetime.

Looking back over Katy's early years, she agreed that "love" was something that she received from her father, and as for the rest of her thoughts, she repeated Uncle Walter's comment, "It is what it is."

Thinking that Katy and I may not always be close friends, I gave Katy a little pink and white jewelry box. As she lifted the lid, a little ballerina started to dance and twirl to the soft music of Tchaikovsky's "Swan Lake"; one of the most popular ballets of our time and the music that we all know so well.

It is the story of a princess who was turned into a swan by an evil sorcerer's curse. The only way that the Princess could be free from this lifelong curse was for someone to step forward and proclaim to love her forever. This was of course the story of Katy as the Princess and Alan as the Prince and their undying brotherly and sisterly love for one another.

Sandra Butler Ladwig

CHAPTER EIGHT

UP IN SMOKE

Louise Palmer was with her mother until she was four years old. She was then put into an Orphanage where she lived until she was 18 years old. In 1958, she moved to Edmonton Alberta, where she married and had four sons. At the age of 41, she was divorced and her four sons had all left home. She was working for a telephone company during the daytime, but her evenings were lonely. She decided that now was the right time for her to find her mother. Louise wrote me a letter asking me for my help in locating her mother. The letter said:

> All I remember is that my Mother's name was Hannah. For days, months and years, I sat looking out the window of the Orphanage waiting and watching for my Mother to come back and get me. I finally realized that she may have died or she had deliberately placed me for adoption. I was never adopted – likely because everybody wanted to adopt babies and not a 4 year old. Either way, I was finally convinced that my Mother was never coming back.

Placed with Social Services at the age of four, I couldn't help but wonder too if Louise's mother had died. Whatever had happened, I was in agreement with Louise that she should find out the truth.

I typed a letter to Social Services in the province where Louise was born, requesting background information on Louise's mother and father, inquiring about their ages, occupations, ethnic origins and whether either had any brothers and sisters. I also asked for information regarding their marital status. If they were married to one another, I asked if there were any other children of the marriage.

I mailed the letter to Louise for her to sign and mail. Six weeks went by. One morning Louise telephoned me asking why she had not yet received a reply. I suggested that she telephone Social Services. Later that day Louise phoned me back, stating that she had been told that her letter was somewhere in a pile of requests on somebody's desk and they would eventually get to it. (Where have we heard that before?)

Four more weeks went by and then another process of telephone calls, only to be given the same answer. All adoptees will relate to this frustrating lapse of time. It is true that the longer a person waits, the more pressing is the need to receive a reply. Seven more weeks went by without a word, and then one morning Louise telephoned me, all excited that she had finally received a reply, and yet disappointed with their answer. The reply stated:

Unfortunately we do not have any information regarding your Mother or your Father. The only information we have is a reference by a social worker to the effect that she thought that you had been placed for adoption, but because you were never adopted, you grew up in an Orphanage. Our records indicate that you were sent to

Sandra Butler Ladwig

an Orphanage at the age of four. The discharge papers signed by the Minister of Social Services were filed when you were 18 years of age.

A shiver went down my spine. "Was this one of those children we hear about that was left on a doorstep?" "Did her mother die?" "Was her father killed overseas?" There were many unanswered questions. All we had to go on was the name "Louise Palmer" and her mother's name, "Hannah Palmer."

I asked Louise if she had a birth certificate. She said she only had a plastic one, with her name, birth date and place of birth on it.

I wrote a letter to Vital Statistics in the province where Louise was born and requested a genealogical paper copy of her birth certificate. I mailed the letter to Louise for her to sign and mail.

Five weeks later Louise telephoned me all excited. She had received her very own birth certificate, and it listed her mother as "Hannah Palmyrucyk." There was no father listed.

That evening I went through all of the telephone books I could find for that province, and I came upon one Edgar Palmyrucyk residing in a small town. I telephoned Mr. Palmyrucyk asking to speak to Hannah. He said, "Hanna is my sister." So as not to perceive myself to be a a strange person or a bill collector, I struck up a bit of a conversation with Edgar. After we chatted for a few minutes, Edgar told me that his sister lives on Vancouver Island." He sounded pleased to give me her telephone number.

I telephoned Louise and told her about my conversation with her Uncle, and gave her Hanna's telephone number. I suggested the manner in which she should approach her mother by telephone. She said she didn't mean to be disrespectful to her Mother and to me, but she refused to telephone Hannah. She asked me if I would telephone Hanna and just open the door for her to follow up with what was supposedly going to originally be a standoff between them because of what Hannah had done. I was reluctant at the time to contact anybody's birth mother for any reason, however, I realized that if I did not make an initial telephone call to Hannah, the truth of why Louise had been placed for adoption would never be revealed.

The next morning I dialled Hannah's telephone number in Victoria. When a lady answered I asked if her name was Hannah. She said, "Yes." I then proceeded to tell her my name and why I was phoning her. I told Hannah all about Louise's initial telephone call to me months ago and I explained how anxious she was to locate her mother that she had not seen since she was 4 years old.

Hannah seemed very kind and yet not at all excited or anxious to hear about Louise. I went on to explain that -ever since Louise had been placed in the Orphanage she had waited and waited for her mother to come back to get her. At that point, Hannah said,

> I had a little girl once and named her Louise Marie. She was born on April 14, 1940. I was told by Social Services that my Louise was mistakenly adopted when she was four years old.

Sandra Butler Ladwig

As we talked, Hannah explained that she had been very ill the first part of 1944 and had to go into the hospital for major surgery. She said she had nobody who could care for her little girl and therefore had no choice but to ask Social Services if they could find a temporary home for Louise Marie for three months. Hannah continued by saying:

> As it turned out I was feeling much better after only two months and so I went back to Social Services and was thrilled to get my baby back. However, they told me that they had had a fire in their office and all of their records were destroyed. Naturally I was devastated.
>
> I contacted the Superintendent and various social workers over the next several years, but I was always told the same thing. They apologized, but concluded that my Louise had likely been mistakenly adopted.
>
> I moved to Vancouver Island and tried to forget about Louise for the time being, but I couldn't. A couple of years later I went home for a visit to see my brother Edgar, and while I was there I went to the Social Services office, which was then in a new building. Again they told me that my original file had been burned in an office fire years ago. The lady said she presumed that Louise Marie had mistakenly been adopted, but they did say that there was hope that perhaps some day Louise may coming looking for information about her adoption, and she would be reunited with me. They therefore asked me to make sure that I always kept their office up to date on my current telephone number and address.

I telephoned Louise and told her all about what Hannah had told me. Louise just hummed and hawed.

"I don't believe what Hannah told you. She is just covering up her transgressions with more lies." (That was a big word with little or no meaning, I thought). Louise continued, "she must have forgotten that she placed me for adoption, or she doesn't want to admit it. She likely made up that story about a fire to cover up the guilt feelings she has had all of these years for just dumping me in an orphanage."

I was not sure what response I expected from Louise, but that was not it! I had not even considered bitterness and accusations. Perhaps growing up in an orphanage had made her hard-hearted. I ended my conversation with Louise by suggesting that she phone Hannah herself, but I wasn't convinced that she would. After I hung up, I felt like someone who had put a whole puzzle together – only to find that the last piece didn't fit, and I concluded that perhaps it never would!

A couple of months later, Louise phoned me and asked if I would come to her house for coffee. She told me that she had gone to Vancouver Island and had met Hannah. "I'm so excited – I have to tell you all about it!"

I was delighted – and wasted no time in finding Louise's house that very evening. Meeting Louise for the first time would be very exciting for me. I had pictured her in my mind several times – tall, dark and attractive.

That evening, I knocked on Louise's door and when she opened it, this person who I had known so well over the telephone, stood before me an absolute stranger. She must not have felt the same way about me, because she grabbed me and hugged me as though she had known me forever.

Sandra Butler Ladwig

Louise was about 5 ft. tall, slight build, with long dark brown hair. We sat at her kitchen table as she showed me photographs of her four boys. Then we started talking about her trip to visit Hannah. I have to tell you first – that I did not let Hannah know that I was coming. I didn't want to give her the opportunity to not be at home.

I flew to Vancouver island last Monday. It took me quite awhile to find Hannah's house by bus. All I had was her street address, but some bus drivers helped me. When I got off the bus I wandered around in circles, checking the street names and house number as I walked from one block to another. Then I stood in front of Hannah's house. It was a large two-storey very old white house with a large veranda on the front.

The three concrete steps up to the front door were awkward to stand on as I reached up and knocked on her door. I wondered if she could hear a knock from inside the main part of her house. I waited and then knocked harder and harder several times. Finally a lady came out to the veranda and opened the door. I had to step back down onto the sidewalk so that she could open the door.

I told her that my name was Louise Marie Palmer. I could see from her great height and large frame that I did not look at all like her. She stared at me, waiting for me to say something more. I told her that I had travelled a long way to see her, and asked if I could come in. She just stood there staring at me. Finally she stepped aside. I then went up the three steps and walked into a large veranda. She shut the door and led me into a living room through old double glass doors.

"You can sit in there." She pointed toward her living room.

At that point I thought that perhaps she did not believe I was her daughter. Also, I was very interested to know why she had placed me for adoption when we had been together for four whole years.

Hannah sat down across from me and waited for me to say something. I didn't know what to say or what to do.

Hannah then stood up and said, "I'll make some tea." She went out to the kitchen and in a few minutes she came into an adjoining room where she sat down some cups and a teapot. (I thought to myself, I will never understand how so many people can get a bang out of drinking coloured hot water.) She asked me to join her at the table.

When we were seated across from one another with a table between us, I felt more comfortable.

To break the ice and get right to the point, I bluntly asked Hannah, "Why did you put me up for adoption?" Hannah did not reply.

I then looked right into her face. Do you have any idea what it was like to grow up in an orphanage; to never be hugged, kissed or tucked into bed at night by your own Mother?" Then I noticed the distance in her eyes that would not let me say anymore.

After a long silence, I told her what little I could remember about my Mother. She stared at me and then told me that she had been very ill when I was four years old and had to have major surgery.

Social Services told me that they would look after you for three months while I was in hospital. When I returned to get you back after only two months, I was told that they had had a fire in their office and that all of their files had been burned. For weeks, months and years after, all the social workers could tell me was that you had likely been mistakenly adopted by someone.

I shook my head at Hannah and just said, 'I don't believe you!'

"Just to keep our conversation lively, I reached into my purse and took out my birth certificate and handed it to Hannah. 'Here!' I said. She unfolded it and seemed to read it over and over again.

She didn't say anything to me, but I was thinking that she was probably contemplating what lie she was going to say next.

Hannah then stood up, went into the living room, opened a drawer, and pulled out something. She returned to the dining room and handed it to me.

I opened an old tattered envelope and unfolded a letter that read in bold print at the top – 'Department of Social Services'. The letter was dated September 4, 1948. It read – 'Several of our files, including the file on you and your daughter were burned in a fire in late 1944. We have no record as to the present whereabouts of your daughter, and can only hope that at some future date we will be able to cross-reference your name and your daughter's name in an effort to reunite the two of you. Please ensure that this office always has an up-to-date address and telephone number of your whereabouts.

The letter was signed by 'A. J. Stevenson, Minister of Social Services.

Louise said that she just shook her head in disbelief or should I say "belief!" She evidently stood up and put her arms around Hannah and said, "We will be together forever now."

Then Hannah stood up, "Just a minute, I have something for you." She went upstairs, and when she returned, she handed me something all bound in tissue paper. She made me promise I would not open it until I got home.

Louise told me that when she got back to the hotel that night she couldn't wait to open the gift. She said that when she unwrapped it, she found a silver locket inside. She opened the silver locket to find that it was a photograph of her when she was four years old.

Author's note: I am sorry. I cannot remember if there was ever any mention of Louise's birth father.

Sandra Butler Ladwig

CHAPTER NINE

WHAT IF SHE SAYS "NO!"

The greatest fear that adoptees have in contacting their birth mothers is their initial response:

"No! I cannot correspond with you;"

"No! I cannot meet you," and

"No! You cannot contact me ever again!"

The reason a birth mother may deny a reunion with her relinquished child is that she may not have told anyone in her family that she had given birth to a baby and then put her baby up for adoption and feels that they would not understand. In a situation such as this, there are many reunions that have taken place in total privacy.

A birth mother also may not want to relive the emotional experience that she had gone through when she was a child herself. Having said that, however, I can promise that I have never met a birth mother who did not love her child or a mother who blames her child for the emotion she had gone through when she was a mere child herself. The advantages of a reunion when her child is grown and when society too has grown, far outweighs any disadvantages. Prior to 1985, unwed mothers wore a fake wedding ring. Some said that the father had died, while others just out and out lied saying whatever they had rehearsed enough that they believed it themselves.

After a birth mother has kept her secret for over 20 years, she may feel that she cannot tell her family now. She may fear that her husband will leave her if he finds out and that her children may lose respect for her or worse yet, disown her. Some husbands are understanding and most children are just happy to know that there is one more out there to love.

It is difficult for an adoptee to understand a negative response, especially when the adoptee grew up in an era where society thought nothing of a single girl raising her baby. The birth mother may have grown up in an era where giving birth to a baby out of wedlock was shameful. "Illegitimate" is not a word that society accepts in this day and age, nor are the words "bastard" or "orphan." After about 1985, parents taught their children to learn and realize that a "child is chosen" and should therefore be looked up to and respected.

Clearly then, an adoptee's initial contact should be to say, "I want you to know that I am fine! I want to thank you for giving birth to me when you may have had other options. I do not want you to have any guilt feelings about placing me for adoption. I have had a good and happy life with wonderful adoptive parents. I do not want you to worry about me."

The adoptee may then communicate her wish to meet her birth mother some day, leaving her name, address and phone number with her birth mother in the event her circumstances may change in the future. If it is a birth mother's request not to be contacted again, the adoptee must then abide by her birth mother's wishes, as hard and difficult as that might be.

The decision on the part of a birth mother to say "no" can be very difficult for an adoptee to accept and to understand, especially if the search for her birth mother had been long, frustrating, painful at times, and expensive.

During the search, an adoptee had likely built up in her mind that wonderful day when she would go running into her birth mother's arms, trading those years of frustration and pain into a lifetime of love and friendship.

Debbie searched for her birth mother daily for six years. She came up against a brick wall several times. Finally, she wrote a letter to Family & Social Services asking if there was anyone who could assist her. A social worker very kindly gave Debbie my name.

I recall that, during my initial telephone call from Debbie, she told me that her adoptive parents were very supportive of her searching for her birth mother. Debbie said that her brother had found his birth mother and he was enjoying a special friendship with her.

Debbie mailed her entire file to me. After reading through it, I could see that she had followed through on just about every idea that I would have had. Her Adoption Order stated that her birth name had been Dianne Sczukalov, a name not difficult to trace.

Her birth date was June 28, 1956. The background information on her birth mother and birth father was as follows:

Birth Mother:

Age:	20.
Occupation:	Store Clerk
Marital Status:	Single
Ethnic Origin:	English
Education:	Grade 10
Complexion:	Medium
Height:	5'-7"
Hair:	Dark Brown

Parents were both deceased at the time of your birth. No brothers or sisters. Her father had been a farmer and her mother a housewife. She enjoyed music, sports and sewing.

Birth Father:

Age:	24
Occupation:	Lumberman
Marital Status:	Single
Ethnic Origin:	English
Complexion:	Medium
Height:	6'
Hair:	Dark Brown
Parents:	(unknown).
Brothers & Sisters:	(unknown).

My first thought was that the name "Sczukalov" was definitely not an English name. From the research Debbie had done, it appeared there were only two Sczukalov families now in Canada: one in Alberta and one in Ontario. The 1956 Edmonton Henderson's Directory showed two Sczukalov families in Edmonton, listed as:

Sczukalov, Arthur, Carpenter, h51 Abbott Avenue

Sczukalov, William (Betty), Chef, h32 Friesen Cr.

Following Arthur and William through the 1960's and 1970's, I could see when each retired, and when they disappeared from the Directories altogether.

The only one remaining was Betty Sczukalov, listed as a widow and still residing as the head of the house at 32 Friesen Crescent.

The Henderson's Directories will have an "r" in front of an address if that person was a "resident," and an "h" if that person was the "head of the house (owner)."

I could see that Debbie had written to Betty Sczukalov asking about Arthur and William. Betty had replied that her husband William had been the only child of Arthur and Mary Sczukalov, and that all three were now deceased.

I also saw where Debbie had written a letter to the hospital where she was born in 1956, requesting a copy of her birth records. Thinking or perhaps knowing that she would never receive them, I was shocked to see in her file an actual copy of Debbie's birth records, where her birth mother's full name was "Louise Dianne Sczukalov." I could see where Debbie again wrote to the hospital asking if they might have an address where her mother was living at the time she gave birth to her. The reply came from a nurse in charge of medical records, demanding an immediate answer to her question, "Were you placed for adoption?"

I could not see where Debbie replied to the nurse. However, the next time Debbie phoned me, I did ask. She told me, "I did not respond to the nurse's letter. However,

I did receive a form letter from an Investigating Officer with our local Police Department requesting information as to why I had tried to get my birth records from the hospital where I was born."

Debbie went on to explain to me that she telephoned the Investigating Officer and explained that she had been adopted and was trying to find out everything she could about her birth mother. The Officer revealed that it was against the law for Debbie to receive medical information from the hospital, especially if she was adopted. Debbie explained to the Officer that she would do anything to find her mother, whether her requests were legal or illegal. Both Debbie and the Officer had a long conversation and then Debbie said that they both had a good laugh about what Debbie had done.

I was not sure where to continue in Debbie's search, other than to think that somewhere in this province there had been a farmer by the name of Sczukalov who had a daughter born about 1936. His daughter had probably attended school from 1942 to 1952, quitting school at age 16, and sometime after that she had met a lumberman.

During the next two months, I went through Church and school records throughout the province, however, I came up empty handed.

One day I stopped in to chat with Betty Sczukalov in person. After I introduced myself, I reminded her of Debbie's letter. Betty was very pleasant and most cooperative. She showed me photographs of her father-in-law Arthur and her husband William.

She then told me that Arthur and his wife Mary had

divorced years ago. Betty assured me that no one in the family had been a farmer, and in fact they had no other relatives in Canada. I asked Betty if they had had a maid, or a close family friend that may have used their surname. She replied, "No! I don't think so."

On the way home, I concluded that Sczukalov was not Debbie's birth mother's maiden name nor her married name. I sat at my table scribbling all kinds of names that Sczukalov could have been derived from, i.e. Szukalovich, Sczukalovitch, Sczukalowoodski, and so on. There had to be some connection with Debbie's surname. About two weeks later, I went back to the library and searched through the Voter's Polls from 1956 to 1960. I noticed that in 1956 Arthur had resided at 51 Abbott Avenue. However, I was astonished to see that he was also listed as a resident in an apartment block at 1025 – 14 Avenue. I went over to City Hall and received the legal description of the property at 1025 – 14 Avenue. I then went over to the Land Titles Office and looked back into the archived Certificates of Title dating back to 1956.

I was surprised to see that Arthur Sczukalov owned the apartment block at 1025 – 14 Avenue. I then went back to the library and looked up the address 1025 – 14 Avenue, writing down the names of all of the residents. Much to my surprise I saw a "Louise D. McKenna" residing in Apartment #205. I very briefly thought that "McKenna" could have been an English surname.

Across the hall from Louise McKenna I noticed a "Florence Creighton." That evening I telephoned Florence Creighton. I asked her if she could possibly remember a Louise McKenna who had lived across the hall from her back in 1956. There was a pause, and then Mrs. Creighton added, "Yes, I do remember her. She and my daughter Julie were good friends." Mrs. Creighton said that her daughter was there visiting with her and that she would pass the phone to her. When Julie came on the phone, I told her that I was trying to locate a Louise McKenna who had lived in apartment #205 back in 1956. She replied "Oh yes! We were good friends up until the time she got married and moved out of the apartment block. I haven't seen her since then."

I decided to tell Julie all about Debbie and her long and frustrating search for her birth mother Louise. I then asked Julie if it was possible that Louise McKenna had had a baby back in 1956. There was a pause, and then Julie replied, "Yes, it seems to me.... Yes, I seem to recall that she had been pregnant back about that time, but we never did see Louise with a baby."

Julie went on to tell me that Louise had attended her wedding in April of 1956. She believed she had a photograph of Louise and her boyfriend. I asked Julie if she had any idea where I could possibly find Louise now. Julie gave me the name of the town where Louise had grown up, but she could not remember Louise's married name. I thanked Julie, and asked if possibly I could drop by sometime and make a copy of the photograph that she had of Louise. She said she could look for the photograph, and asked that I give her two weeks to find it before I dropped by. I thanked her for her assistance and kindness and agreed to phone her back in two weeks.

That evening I telephoned Debbie to bring her up to date on everything I had learned. It was difficult to convince her that her birth mother's legal name had been McKenna when she had believed for six long years that her name and her birth mother's name was Sczukalov.

I asked Debbie to send me some photographs of herself at various stages of her growing up years. I wanted to compare Debbie's photographs to the one photograph that Julie had of Louise McKenna.

The next day, I took the telephone book and looked for the name "McKenna" in the small town that Julie had mentioned. I saw a Don McKenna listed and I telephoned him. I simply asked him if he could give me Louise's phone number. Mr. McKenna was very kind and polite. He not only gave me Louise's telephone number, he added, "her married name is "Manning."

That afternoon I telephoned Louise Manning. When she answered, I asked if she could possibly assist me in locating the family of Arthur Sczukalov. I went on to say that he had been her landlord at 1025 – 14 Avenue back in the mid-1950's.

Mrs. Manning replied softly, "I don't think so. I did live in that apartment block. However, I don't remember ever meeting the landlord or any other tenants who lived there."

I then asked if she possibly remembered Arthur's daughter Louise Diane Sczukalov. (It is difficult to hear if anyone is startled or shocked on the other end of a telephone.) Louise replied, "I paid my rent by mail and don't remember ever meeting anyone in that apartment block." I knew that was a lie because Louise had been good friends with Julie Creighton who lived across the hall from her.

I continued as though I did not hear her response, "I would very much like to contact Arthur's daughter regarding a very pleasant, personal matter." Louise then clarified, "I don't remember that Mr. Sczukalov had a daughter. I don't remember that he had any family at all." Well, now I knew she was lying so perhaps I was getting somewhere.

I continued talking about apartment living, hoping that Louise may warm up to our almost one-sided conversation. I could sense that she seemed upset all of a sudden. Not wanting to press her any further, I thanked her for speaking with me. I said goodbye and hung up.

I sat by my phone pondering over my conversation with Louise Manning. First she claimed that she had never met her landlord, and yet later on, she seemed to know that Arthur did not have a daughter. When she told me that she had never met anyone in that apartment block, had she forgotten about Julie Creighton and Julie's mother Florence who lived across the hall?

I received six very lovely photographs from Debbie. About three weeks later, I stopped by the library and made a photocopy of the McKenna family history from the history book of the town where Louise had grown up. The family had originated from England at the turn of the Century. I found it interesting that Louise McKenna Manning had four brothers and five sisters whereas Louise Diane Sczukalov had no brothers and no sisters.

There is a reason why birth mothers will lie about the birth and relinquishment of their babies, and that is because they are afraid that one half of society will tell the other half of society about the crime they committed. One half of society will judge them and the other half of society will be the jury, both proclaiming a birth mother to be a shameful person. It sometimes takes a long time for a birth mother to stand up straight and learn to respect herself again. Dr. Phil said, "Never let anybody tell you who you are!" Yet we all do it. Kahlil Gibran put it nicely in one of his poems where he tells of a birth mother who conceived her child because of love and affection; she gave birth to her child through pain and suffering; and then she went to the orphanage, leaving her baby there and as she ascended the orphanage steps – you and I taunted her, "For Shame." "For Shame." Well, we don't do that anymore.

I telephoned Mrs. Creighton and asked if I could come to her home to meet with her and her daughter Julie. She said they would be pleased to meet me. I picked up donuts and arrived at their house about an hour later. I was greeted most hospitably by both Florence and Julie Creighton. We talked in general for about half an hour, and then our conversation switched to Debbie and her search for her birth mother. I again told them all about Debbie and her years of searching – her desire, and her dreams of some day finding her first mother. I then showed them the six photographs of Debbie.

Julie said, "By the way, I found the photograph of Louise McKenna and her boyfriend." She handed the photograph to me. I studied it and noticed that Louise was about seven months pregnant in that photograph. Comparing the photographs, I was delighted to see that Debbie looked a lot like Louise McKenna. I was think-

The Tigers in Your Dreams   173

ing that the man with Louise was likely Debbie's birth father.

I was just about to ask Julie if I could take the photograph and make a copy of it, when she handed it to me, "Here – take the photograph and send it to your friend Debbie." I thanked Florence and Julie for their hospitality and left their home late that afternoon.

The next day I telephoned Louise McKenna Manning. As I could hear her phone ringing, I realized I had no idea what I was about to say to her. When she answered, I said, "I don't know if you remember me or not. I telephoned you a few weeks ago about Arthur Sczukalov and his family. I wonder, since my last call, if you may have remembered something about that family?"

She replied, "No! Like I said, I don't remember that he had any family at all."

I then proceeded to tell her all about Debbie, born as Dianne Sczukalov on June 28, 1956, and her long and frustrating search for her birth mother. I continued telling her of Debbie's desire to locate her Mother and become friends with her. Again Louise repeated her words, "I never did know anyone who lived in that apartment block, so I wouldn't have known her."

I then asked Louise, "Do you not remember Julie Creighton, who lived just across the hall from you? Evidently you and she were good friends." I continued, pressing harder, "Don't you remember going to Julie's wedding in April of 1956? At that point I could hear Louise crying. Still sobbing, she said, "I have something to tell you."

"Now, now." I said in a consoling voice. "I did not

mean to upset you. Debbie just wants to know that her search is over. She does not intend on hurting you in any way." At that point, I was thinking to myself that – here is a birth mother who wishes to retain her privacy and leave her past in the past.

"I can't see her." Louise said softly. "Nobody knows about her!"

There was a pause in our conversation, and then I said, "I do have six photographs of Debbie. Would you like to see them?"

We made arrangements to meet one another in a restaurant the next morning. I noticed her as soon as I walked into the restaurant. Once seated I saw that she was a very pretty lady. We talked for a bit – and then I handed her Debbie's photographs. She asked me if she could keep them. As she was putting them into her purse, I asked Louise where she was going to hide them from her family. She told me that she had a very special place in mind.

I thought that seeing the photographs would entice Louise into wanting to see Debbie. However, it did the exact opposite. She was satisfied. This is why I have always told adoptees to never send photographs to their birth mothers unless it is in person.

Debbie did telephone Louise one evening, however, Louise asked her not to telephone her again. Debbie promised she would not telephone her again, providing Louise would phone her every six months, just to tell her how she was doing. During the next two years Debbie did not hear from Louise.

One day Debbie's husband said "That's it! We are

going up to Edmonton to see Louise." He drove up to Edmonton and then to Louise's office. Debbie went into her birth mother's office. Once Louise realized who she was, she motioned for Debbie to sit down. Only about ten minutes later, Louise stood up and motioned for Debbie to stand up as well. Louise put out her arm in a gesture to guide Debbie to the doorway. Louise did hug Debbie and then she left.

Many years later after no telephone calls from Louise, Debbie and her husband decided to go up to Louise's son's law office, pretending to want to hire a lawyer. Once they talked about the legalities of opening a new business, Debbie confessed, "I came to see you about one other thing. I came to see you about you being my brother."

Debbie explained the entire situation to her brother and then he said, "I remember a telephone call one evening that Mom would not explain to me. Now I know that had to be you on the telephone."

Debbie and her brother secretly keep in touch with one another every six months, however, there has been no contact with Louise, which is the way Louise wanted it.

Unfortunately there are times when a birth mother will refuse contact with her birth child.

When a birth mother and her child meet and become friends, all of the regret, guilt and painful emotions will fade away forever. This true story about Debbie and Louise is proof that the Tigers in your dreams will never catch you unless you run away. Sad to say, there has never been any mention of Debbie's birth father. Sometimes birth fathers want to marry the mother of their soon-to-be

Sandra Butler Ladwig

child, but the mothers refuse. Perhaps Debbie's father knew about Debbie and would love to know all about her, but has no idea how to go about it. Perhaps a DNA kit could help out.

CHAPTER TEN

A HOLE IN
MY HEART

(As told to me by Bill Tolmie)

Me and my two brothers were standing by the Community Centre the day our dad phoned the authorities on us. We heard him say that the seven of us were too young to be left alone while Mom was in the hospital giving birth to an eighth child. Mervin 8 years old, Harold 9, and I, being 11 at the time, were left to look after the four youngest. We also heard Dad say that Mother was unfit to care for any of us kids. The oldest of us knew that Mom drank, but Dad made it sound so terrible over the phone that day. It was never as bad as he made it sound. Dad didn't want any part of us. He had left us about six months before, but some of us saw him lurking about now and then. Later that day a man and a woman, who said they were Social Workers, arrived at our house and took all of us to a big building downtown. We were told that our Mom would be in hospital for quite some time. They told us that we had a new baby brother named "Todd," but one Social Worker said he had a hole in his heart and would likely not live any more than a day or two. We were all split up that day. It was the scariest and saddest day of my life.

I was sent to an institution, much like an orphanage, up on the northern tip of the island, where I lived for the next six years. When I was 17 years old, I got a job in a logging camp. I learned all about milling. I saved most of my money in the hope that some day I would have my own lumber mill. I married when I was 22 years old to a wonderful girl named Gwen.

When I was 24 years old, Gwen and I set out on holidays in an effort to locate my two brothers and four sisters. We went to my home town and decided to begin by visiting relatives to see if they knew anything that would help us in our search. I was so happy to find that one aunt had raised my sister Nellie, and another aunt had raised Sarah and Jane, but nobody knew where to find our baby sister Susan. Both of my aunts told me that they had tried to get Susan, but they were told that the government had placed her for adoption.

The only thing they knew about Mervin and Harold was that they had been sent to an orphanage or home for boys up north somewhere. They also told me that they believed Mom was still alive and living somewhere in the interior of B.C. They also thought dad was still alive, but they had no idea where he lived.

After visiting with my sisters for a few days, Gwen and I drove up the island, stopping in every town questioning oldtimers about orphanages or homes for boys. Finally, we arrived at Parksville. Gwen went into the bank to get some money while I went over to a pay phone to check the telephone directory for the names Mervin or Harold

Tolmie. Neither name was listed. As I was walking back to the car, I saw Gwen hurrying along back to the car with such excitement.

Breathlessly she said, "If I didn't know better, I would say that you are working over there in that bank."

I grabbed Gwen's arm and we rushed into the bank. I stood there all out of breath; my eyes gazing into the faces of every person behind the counter. Suddenly I saw him. As I started walking toward him, he looked directly at me.

"May I help you?" he asked

All I could think of saying was, "Do I know you from somewhere?"

He replied, "I was about to ask you the same thing."

"My name is Bill Tolmie Is your last name Tolmie?" I questioned hopefully.

"It was at one time."

"Are you Mervin or Harold?" I asked.

"Mervin," he said, grinning from ear to ear.

"I can't believe it is really you."

"Just a minute, I'm going to see if I can have the rest of the day off. He turned and walked into an office behind him and when he came out, he nodded.

Mervin came out from behind the counter and the three of us left together. Once we were outside of the bank, we threw our arms around one another, hugged, and we both shed a few tears.

After introducing Mervin to my wife, I asked if he had any idea where Harold might be."

"Oh sure! We were adopted by the same family.

He just works over there at Sears in the Men's Wear Department."

"Can we go and see him?" I asked excitedly. We walked over to Sears. I remember that my heart was pounding so loud that I could almost hear it. This was beginning to feel more exciting than Christmas morning.

We walked into the store and found men's wear right away. The three of us stood on our tip toes looking over racks of clothes. Then Mervin pointed, "There he is over there!"

"You go first," I said to Mervin.

Mervin approached Harold, and when Harold said "Hi," Mervin stood back, reached out his arm, and said to Harold, "I have somebody I want you to meet."

Harold looked at me, and with an astonished look on his face, he said, "It can't be!" "Is it really you Bill?"

"It sure is." I replied as I ran to him and threw my arms around him.

That was the greatest day – the day I found my three sisters and my two brothers. Now all that was missing was our little sister Susan. Hopefully she will come and find us some day. (If she should read this story, her birth name is "Susan Tolmie.")

****

A HOLE IN HIS HEART

(This part of the story was written by me, Sandra)

It was a Thursday evening in January 1990, the day that a young man phoned me, asking if I would help him find his mother. He sounded so sad and so alone.

His name was Todd Tolmie. I really mean it. He really did sound sad and alone over the telephone if that is possible.

"I am a foster child," he said. "I have lived in three foster homes; one until I was 8 years old, another until I was 12, and I left the last one when I was 17. I was told that my mom gave me away, but I don't know why. She didn't even place me for adoption. It was just like she didn't care if I had a home or not." Todd went on to say that he knew nothing about his father. "I have no brothers or sisters, no aunts, uncles or cousins. I have no one. I would like to find out why my mother didn't want me."

I assured him, "Of course your mother wanted you! She was possibly not married when you were born, and maybe she had no way of supporting you. Perhaps she was very ill at the time you were born. There could be many reasons why you were not raised by your mother, but it would never be because she didn't love and want you!"

Todd went on to tell me that he was born with a hole in his heart and that he had had numerous operations up to the age of five. At that point I added that it was possible that his mother did love him enough to place him for adoption, but because of the hole in his heart, the government could have determined him to be "Unadoptable."

I asked Todd if he had a birth certificate. "Only the little wallet-sized one," he replied. I suggested we send for his long paper birth certificate that would show the name of his mother and father and their places of birth. We filled out the appropriate form to order his birth cer-

Sandra Butler Ladwig

tificate and sent along the $25.00 fee. Four weeks later, Todd received a reply that they were unable to provide him with his birth certificate without the names of his mother and father on the order form.

Since Todd was born in a small city in the B.C. interior, we wrote a letter to the only hospital in that city – asking for a copy of his birth records and any medical records they may have relative to his heart operations. The reply from a doctor in that city stated, "Under the circumstances, we would only be able to forward the birth and medical information to your doctor."

Our next step was to find a doctor that would send for that information on Todd's behalf. We went to see a doctor at the local clinic. However, he refused to send for the information because he stated that he did not believe in a child searching for a biological mother, adopted or not!

Todd was lonely enough as it was. These doors closing, and brick walls did nothing for his hope for the future and let's put it this way – his faith in mankind.

One evening I looked up the name Tolmie in the small city where Todd was born. There were four listings. I struck out on the first three, but on the fourth call, after explaining about Todd searching for his mother, the lady said "I am related to a Bill Tolmie on Vancouver Island. He was from a large family who were all separated when they were very young." She went on to explain that Bill had searched for and found all of his brothers and sisters. She said that she did not believe there was a person in that family by the name of Todd.

After I hung up, I sat by the phone thinking I had

struck out again. Then an interesting thought came to mind. "What if Bill Tolmie, during his search for his brothers and sisters, might have come across a family missing a son, a brother or a nephew named Todd?"

I looked through all of the phone books I could find for towns and cities on Vancouver Island, and only came up with one Bill Tolmie. Since it was very late and I was beginning to worry about the size of my phone bill, I sat down that very evening and wrote a letter to Bill Tolmie, sealed it, kissed it, and dropped it in a nearby mailbox.

Author's Note: We were taught in school that it is against all rules of writing to take on two points of view at the same time, however, I am going to follow my heart and move you to the home of Bill Tolmie, who owns a lumber mill across the street from his home, where he comes home for lunch every day.

A week after I mailed the letter to Bill Tolmie it arrived in his mailbox. Gwen made lunch for her husband Bill, who would be home soon. While she was waiting for him, she stepped out to her front porch and took the mail out of the mailbox. Bill arrived home for lunch and sat down at the kitchen table, with his lunch laid out before him.

Gwen said, "Looks like you got a letter from a woman!" She waved the sealed envelope in his face, giggling as she did it. Bill said, "Open it up and read it to me while I eat my lunch." The letter read:

I have a friend named Todd Tolmie, who phones me often. Todd is a foster child, having lived in three different homes. He is in search of his mother, who may or may not have placed him for adoption. Todd was never adopted – possibly because he had a hole in his heart when he was born and therefore required several operations at a very young age.

Todd is a very lonely young man, trying desperately to find his place in this world. Whenever he phones me, we talk for a couple of hours. I always try to give him hope that some day we will find his mother and he may then have some relatives. Many of us take for granted having a mother and father, brothers and sisters, aunts, uncles and cousins, but Todd has no one.

I understand from one of your aunts that you were separated from your brothers and sisters when you were very young. Your aunt told me that you searched for and found all of your brothers and sisters a few years ago. What I am wondering Bill is, during your search for your family did you ever come across anyone missing or searching for a son, a brother, or a nephew by the name of Todd Tolmie?

P.S. I can assure you he is a very kind, wonderful person. He has just lost his way and is need of finding his own family.

Gail looked up to see tears rolling down Bill's face. "What is it?" she asked, extremely concerned.

Bill replied through his tears, "Todd is my little baby brother that the doctors said would not survive any longer than a day or two. He was born with a hole in his heart."

Back to my house in Alberta, Bill wasted no time in phoning me. All I could hear was someone on the other end of the telephone crying. Finally he told me he was

Bill Tolmie, and that Todd was his little baby brother. He went on to explain the entire story to me.

After Bill hung up, I phoned Todd. I said, "You better sit down!"

"Okay, I'm sitted!" he replied giggling at himself.

Then I proceeded. "I found your family! You have three brothers and four sisters. I just spoke with your brother Bill. He was so excited he was crying. He did say that your Mother is still alive, and he knows where she lives. Your father is believed to still be alive too, although he doesn't know where he is."

I could hear Todd gasping on the other end of the telephone, and his voice broke now and then as though he were trying to hold back tears. "I am so happy."

I told Todd everything Bill had told me and gave him Bill's phone number. I slept very peacefully that night, but I was sure the Tolmie family would be awake most or all night.

The next day there was a knock at my front door, and when I opened it, a florist handed me a huge bouquet of flowers from Bill Tolmie & Family. Not an hour later, I opened the door again to receive a dozen long stemmed red roses from Todd.

A few weeks later, Todd drove out to Vancouver Island and met all of his brothers and sisters for the first time. I too have had the pleasure of meeting Bill, Gwen and Mervin. Todd comes by to visit me every few months, never letting me forget how happy he is, and that he has now literally and realistically repaired the hole in his heart!

Author's note: In the story "What is it like to Hear a Hand," Uncle Harry's daughter Debbie works with Gwen Tolmie. Small world!

Chapter Eleven

LOOKING OVER MY SHOULDER
(and don't do this at home!)

Tony McIntyre phoned me from Leduc one morning, asking if I could help him find his baby sister. He said that he was one of seven children placed for adoption or into foster care 32 years ago after their parents were killed in a car accident. Three of the children were sent to New York to be adopted, two of the older children were placed in foster homes in Alberta, and the little baby girl Marion Marie McIntyre was placed for adoption in Alberta. Fortunately six of the children found one another in recent years. However, they all felt that their family would not be complete without finding Marion.

I advised Tony that there were only two places where he could find information about his sister Marion, and those were: (1) in the Department of Social Services, and (2) at the Department of Vital Statistics.

Tony told me that he was going to go to Vital Statistics to see if anyone would assist him in finding Marion's adopted name and the names of her adoptive parents.

He was sure that her adoptive parents would not mind if Marion met her six brothers and sisters.

A few days passed before Tony phoned me again. He told me what had happened.

> I went down to the Department of Vital Statistics yesterday, which is located on the second floor of a government building. I asked the girl behind the counter if I could receive a copy of my sister's birth certificate. The girl provided me with a form to fill out. I filled in Marion's full name, her birth date, place of birth and the names of our parents.
>
> I then went back to the counter and handed the form back to the girl. She took the form and said she would be right back. About 10 minutes later she returned with the form and information she had written on a small piece of paper. She was about to provide me with the information she had found when, all of a sudden, she asked, 'Was your sister adopted?'
>
> Tony said that he didn't know how to reply, except to confess, "I don't know!" The girl then said, 'I'm sorry, I can't give you this information.'
>
> She took the little piece of paper, ripped it up, and threw it down under the counter – probably into her waste paper basket.

Tony said that he returned home feeling extremely disappointed that he had been so close to finding out his sister's adopted name and the names of her adoptive parents.

Then the next day I was astonished and shocked when

he proceeded to tell me something that he had done that would help us get the information we needed.

> Last night at about 5:30 p.m. I went back to the Department of Vital Statistics. Since the building was closed, I just stood at the doorway looking around. Then I saw a man that looked like he could be a janitor. I knocked on the window.

> The janitor looked up. Then I waved him over to the door. At first the janitor shook his head, and then I motioned for him to open the door, even a wee bit.

> The janitor opened the door, questioning me. I told him that I had been hired as a Janitor's Helper and was to start work at 5:30 p.m. The janitor said that he had not been told about this. I then nonchalantly replied that likely his boss had not been able to get hold of him to tell him about me. The janitor then let me in the door.

Tony asked where he should start. The janitor gave him a handful of garbage bags and told him,

> Go up to the second floor and empty all of the garbage containers in each of the private offices and then in the general office area into these garbage bags. When you are finished, bring the garbage bags down there to the back door, and line them up along the wall there. When all of the garbages are emptied here on the main floor take them to the back door as well. When you are finished, prop open the back door and take all of the bags out to the garbage bin to the left of the back door.

Tony said that he nodded, tucked the garbage bags under his arm and headed for the stairs. Once upstairs, he immediately went to the garbage container under the counter of the girl who had waited on him that morning. He emptied it into one bag, blew air into the bag to make it look full, and then scrunched the top and tied it around his finger.

He then emptied several garbage containers into second and third bags. He held the first bag tight in the fist of his left hand, grabbed the second and third bags with his right hand and headed down to the back door on the main floor. As he turned to go toward the back door, he peered left and then right, but did not see the janitor anywhere. He walked down a hallway that led to the back door, almost holding his breath for fear of hearing his name called. Afraid to look back, Tony opened the back door, walked out into the dark laneway, dropped the second and third bags into a garbage bin, and then dashed to his car. He threw his garbage bag into the front passenger seat of his car, jumped in, and drove away.

He said he kept looking in his rear-view mirror cautiously and quietly, with the fear of a criminal who had just robbed a bank. He did not breathe a sigh of relief until he drove into his own garage at Leduc.

Once inside his house, he yelled for his wife to come and help him. He told his wife breathlessly what he had done. She stood in total disbelief.

Tony carefully emptied the garbage bag onto his living room carpet. He remembered the size of the paper the girl had ripped up. He carefully handled each piece of paper, discarding the larger pieces. Finally he was left with small pieces of paper that he carefully put together like a puzzle.

On the phone to me that day, Tony revealed, "I have

her adopted name and the names of her adopted parents." As he read them to me, I carefully wrote down the words, "Elizabeth Ann Carter, Marie Carter and Jeff Carter, Athabasca."

I was delighted to hear the name Athabasca, as I had just completed a search for an adoptee named Jean who lived in Athabasca. I was sure that Jean could assist me because she had lived in Athabasca all her life. I told Tony I would phone him back in an hour.

I phoned Jean, telling her all about the seven children split up and the search for their baby sister. "Yes," she exclaimed. "Yes, I know Elizabeth and both of her parents very well." Knowing there was a right and a wrong way to approach this very delicate matter, I asked Jean if she knew what Church the Carters attended. She told me that they attend the United Church, and then she provided me with the name and phone number of their Minister – Rev. Mark Sands.

I phoned Tony, telling him to phone Reverend Sands and what to say to him. After explaining the situation to the Reverend, I suggested that Reverend Sands contact Mr. and Mrs. Carter asking them if he could visit with them regarding a personal matter. I felt sure Mr. and Mrs. Carter would not mind if their 21 year old daughter met her six brothers and sisters. I waited three days before Tony phoned me back.

He told me that Reverend Sands had visited with Mr. and Mrs. Carter, and when he told them about Elizabeth's six brothers and sisters wanting to meet her, they were furious because they said, "When we adopted Elizabeth, we asked if she had any brothers and sisters we could

Sandra Butler Ladwig

adopt as well. The Social Worker told us that Elizabeth was an only child."

As for meeting her brothers and sisters, Mr. and Mrs. Carter agreed that they would leave that decision up to Elizabeth. The very next morning, Mr. and Mrs. Carter phoned Tony. They spoke to him briefly and then handed the phone to Elizabeth.

Tony told me that their conversation had been extremely emotional. Plans were then made for them to meet the next day.

About two weeks later, which was right after Christmas, Tony phoned me to tell me that he and his six brothers and sisters, all of their children, and all of the adoptive parents and foster parents rented a small hall to spent Christmas Day together. He also told me that each set of parents went up to a small stage individually and told about how much happiness their child had brought to their lives. After they were finished, the adoptive and foster parents all went up onto the stage together and they all expressed that they now considered themselves to have seven children, rather than one, and how blessed each of them were.

When you drive on the QE2 into Leduc from the south, right there over "the rise," if you crouch down a bit and cautiously and quietly look over your shoulder to the east, you will see Tony's house.

CHAPTER TWELVE

VICTORIA'S SECRET

Three years ago when I completed this search, I said then – that I would never tell anybody this story. There were too many lies and too much deception that I could never divulge to anyone. Now, thinking about the miracle of it all, I am not only telling Victoria's story, I am telling the whole story just as it happened. Victoria had a secret indeed.

This search began the day I received a letter from a young lady named Jennifer, seeking assistance in locating her birth mother. She enclosed her Adoption Order and Background Information. Her letter was filled with an urgent plea that I find her birth mother in time for her to attend her upcoming wedding. She went on to explain that her parents had been encouraging her to search for her birth parents since she was 17 years old, and now at the age of 23, she wanted to find them too.

Jennifer explained in her letter that she had been a bit of a renegade in her teens, behaving unruly and irresponsible. She was not exactly the kind of child typical of adoptive parents who were both United Church Ministers. "My parents and I are as different as cheese and chalk." She said that her parents likely thought that if she found her birth mother back in her teens, she may settle down and their problems with her would be over.

With interest, I looked at her Adoption Order. At the top, it read simply, "Jennifer." There was no surname! I scanned down to her birth date, and my heart sank when I read "September 4, 1966." In Alberta, the surname of an adoptee was extracted from the Adoption Order on all adoptions made legal between March of 1965 and December of 1985. I would not even have begun this search without a surname had Jennifer not been born here in Red Deer; the city where I live. I thought, "It can't be that hard to find her birth mother in a city this size." The background information would surely give me good clues.

> In 1966 her birth mother was 23 years of age
> Single
> Born in Quebec
> English
> Religion – United
> Completed Grade 11 at 18 years of age
> Occupation: Medical Secretary
> Medium height, 130 lbs.,
> Fair complexion, green eyes and blonde hair
> Interests included music, art, reading and outdoor sports.
> She played the organ and piano.
> Her parents were separated – both lived in Alberta
> Her father was an auto mechanic
> She had one married sister
> Your birth mother had known your birth father for 9 years.

I would have been worried about her mother being born in Quebec, as a birth mother will actually travel across the country, give birth, and then travel back to her home, except for the fact that it stated her birth parents both lived in Alberta. That gave me some hope that perhaps her whole family had moved here.

In 1966 her birth father was 40 years of age
Married
Born in Quebec
Educational standing – Grade 12.
Religion – United
Service station manager
Height – 6', 200 lbs., fair complexion,
Deep set blue eyes, blonde hair,
High forehead
His parents live in Quebec; his father was retired.
He was an only child.

Since Jennifer's birth father was born in Quebec and his parents lived in Quebec, I wondered if Jennifer had been conceived in Quebec, but I quickly dismissed that idea because of the one statement that revealed, "She had known your birth father for 9 years." I wondered in what capacity they had known one another for 9 years. She would have been only 14 years old and in Grade 8 when they met, and he would have been 31. Since Jennifer's maternal grandfather had been an auto mechanic and her birth father had been a service station manager, perhaps they had been business associates.

Certainly if a 23 year old girl were dating a 40 year old married man here in this city, somebody must have known, and why was she dating a married man?

The first step was to speak to my own husband Fred, who was an auto mechanic and had lived here since he was a child. I asked him if he knew a service station manager who would now be about 64 years old, 6 ft. in height, 200 lbs., who was born in Quebec. He said, "I remember a Frenchman who ran a service station downtown near the Safeway store, but I can't remember his name."

I then went to the library and photocopied a list of service stations in the 1966 Henderson's Directory, which also showed the names of the managers or owners, but none of them sounded French. I showed the list to Fred, but he could not pinpoint the service station he had in mind when we first spoke.

I placed an advertisement in two Friday editions in the Personal column of our local newspaper. It read, "Adoptee – Jennifer – Born September 4, 1966 – seeking assistance in locating my birth mother. Reply Box 35, c/o the newspaper." There were no replies to that personal ad.

My next step was to contact some medical secretaries I knew who were in their 50's. I felt that the only way to find out the information I was seeking was to tell each of them the truth. Unfortunately, none of the medical secretaries I spoke with could remember anyone from the description of Jennifer's birth mother.

I drew a graph of our birth mother's life: when she was born, when she started school, when she quit school, when she gave birth to Jennifer, and when she might have married. I couldn't find her birth without a surname; I couldn't find her starting school without her surname.

Possibly many girls quit school in Grade 11 that year. I couldn't find out who she married without her surname. That left only: the occasion of Jennifer's birth. There were only three places that knew Jennifer's birth name; (1) the Department of Child & Family Services, (2) the Department of Vital Statistics, and (3) our local hospital where Jennifer was born.

I drove past the hospital several times that week, and thinking as some adoptees do, I wondered if I could get a job in Medical Records. When I had the information I wanted, I would simply quit. "No!" I shook that idea from my head. But, if I only had a friend there who would help me.

That evening I telephoned my doctor at home and asked her if she could help. She said that she unfortunately does not have access to old hospital medical records.

There was little else to do but write a letter to the Administrator of the hospital, appealing to his sensitivity of a mother and child separated for 23 years. I mailed the letter to Jennifer and asked her to sign it and mail it to the Hospital Administrator. Her letter remained unanswered a month later.

I telephoned the Administrator's office and asked for an appointment Friday morning at 9:00 a.m. The receptionist asked for the nature of my visit. I told her it was very personal, and I wished only to speak to the Administrator. I would not have been so secretive, except that I knew that if I told the receptionist the truth, she would have turned me away in that phone call, and if the Administrator himself had known, he would have done the same. Therefore, I kept the reason for my visit a secret until I was sitting across the table from him that following Friday morning at 9:00 a.m.

"What can I do for you?" he asked with interest. I was afraid to even begin because I knew in my heart he would deny my request and abruptly end our meeting.

I first reminded him of Jennifer's letter, showing him a photocopy of it for authenticity. I told him of my assistance in helping Jennifer with her search, and could he possibly release her birth surname either to me or to Jennifer. I added, "It's not fair to those born after 1965 when those born prior to 1965 receive their surname. Jennifer was a patient in this hospital, and therefore has a right to her medical records, don't you think?"

The administrator replied, "You have to understand my position. If Jennifer's birth mother wanted to keep Jennifer's birth a secret and found out that I released that confidential information to you or to Jennifer, she could cause a lot of problems for this hospital."

I pleaded with the Administrator to trust my judgment and my experience. However, regardless of my background and my promises, he was definite that he would not entrust Jennifer's surname to her nor to me.

Then I asked him, "Would you consider searching for Jennifer's birth mother yourself and ask her if she would like to meet Jennifer?"

"I wouldn't even know how to begin," he replied.

"I could teach you how to search for her, giving you step by step directions – would you please? It doesn't matter who finds her or how she is found, as long as somebody asks her if she would like to see her daughter again."

I pleaded with him, and if my face showed that plea, that would have been the reason why he agreed. I told him I would write him a letter giving him directions on how to begin a search for Jennifer's birth mother.

That evening I typed a letter to the Administrator, asking him if he would obtain the name of Jennifer's birth mother from the September 4, 1966 hospital records. Then I told him to take that name down to the Public Library and ask for the 1966, 1967 and 1968 Henderson's Directories. "Look up that name in those old Directories and see if you can see who she was living with by the same surname. The listing will show the birth mother with an "r" beside her name and an "h" beside her parents' names. The "r" means "resident" and the "h" means "head of the house." Then look in the current Henderson's Directory for the address and phone number of her parents.

Then please place a telephone call to each of them. They will be able to give you their daughter's married name and telephone number. If that doesn't work, go back to the 1966 Henderson's Directory. Make a note of the birth mother's address and then turn to the back of the Directory and look up that address. It will show who the birth mother's neighbours were. Make a note of the names of the neighbours and then go to the current telephone book and phone one or all of the neighbours, who are hopefully still living here in Red Deer. Ask them if they know where Jennifer's birth mother and her parents are now living. (The person who is searching has to put themselves in the position of the birth mother, and of course use their own common sense.)

I waited six weeks with no reply from the Administrator. I decided to contact him, but before I did, I phoned Jessie, a friend of mine who was a good friend of the Supervisor of Motor Vehicles. I asked Jessie for the Supervisor's name, business address and telephone number.

I then phoned the Administrator. He sounded very busy when he answered the telephone, hastily saying, "I tried all I could, but have been unable to locate Jennifer's birth mother or any of her family." I thanked him for his effort, and advised him that I would be sending him instructions on how to take the next step.

Knowing that he had Jennifer's birth mother's full name, I assumed he had found out the names of her grandparents also. I wrote a letter to the Administrator asking him to contact Mrs. Francis Adams, the Supervisor of the Department of Motor Vehicles, asking for her assistance in searching for Jennifer's maternal grandparents. It is possible that both of them still drive a vehicle and that each has an Operator's License with their current addresses on them.

I gave the Administrator Mrs. Adams telephone number at Motor Vehicles. I assumed that Jennifer's birth mother would likely be married, and not knowing her married name, Mrs. Adams could not check for an Operator's License for her. However, she could check out the names of Jennifer's grandparents. I mailed the letter and again waited for his reply.

Waiting is very difficult for adoptees, and therefore I

took my own advice and purchased a 3-ring binder. The first title page would read "Jennifer's Search for her Birth Mother," followed by Jennifer's adoption documents and copies of all correspondence. I also included hand-written notations of my thoughts and all of my telephone calls. I would continue adding to the album with every effort I made.

Six weeks later, I telephoned the Administrator, not knowing what to suggest next without knowing what he had found out so far. I was a little discouraged because Jennifer's wedding day had come and gone without her birth mother in attendance. However, I decided not to tell the Administrator that, as he may think that the search is not as important nor even necessary now.

The Administrator said, "I am waiting for some information from Mrs. Adams." We thought we were getting somewhere, but the person in Calgary we were trying to contact is away on business. We will keep trying."

Two weeks later I had an idea that perhaps Vital Statistics, who holds birth, death and marriage records, may release information to the Administrator of a hospital. I telephoned Vital Statistics to inquire, and it appeared that they would release the information to him, but only over the telephone. The girl asked me, "What is the name, and I will do the search for you if you wish to hold on."

Of course I did not have the surname, but told her I would have the Hospital Administrator phone her. I wrote a letter to the Administrator suggesting that he try that route, giving him the telephone number for Vital Statistics.

Three weeks later I contacted the Administrator once again. He told me that he had tried Vital Statistics, but they would not release any information to him. He went on to say that all of his efforts to Alberta Health Care, the tax department and a contact in Calgary had been futile. He ended our entire relationship by saying, "I have tried all I can. I wish you luck in your next search!"

It bothered me that he knew all of the names and addresses of the people I wanted so desperately to know, and now, without his help, I was back at square one.

I pondered and thought and connived and plotted. Then I did the most unforgivable thing at that point, as though I personally had no ethics whatsoever. I contacted Mrs. Francis Adams of the Department of Motor Vehicles. I mentioned our mutual friend Jessie and then asked if I could talk to her in person about a confidential matter. Since Mrs. Adams and I had a mutual friend Jessie, she agreed, suggesting I come to her home.

That evening I drove to the home of Francis Adams and knocked on her door, not knowing if she would be receptive or not once she knew the reason for my visit. When she opened the door she introduced herself to me, ushered me into her den, and we sat comfortably across from one another.

"Now then, what can I do for you," she asked.

I refreshed her memory about her association with the Administrator of the hospital. I told her all about Jennifer, the support of her adoptive parents, and the fact that Jennifer did not even know her own birth name while thousands of other adoptees, born prior to 1965, knew their birth names.

I told her about every effort that had been made to find Jennifer's birth mother. She responded, "I can't remember the surname offhand. There are so many names that come across my desk during the course of a day, but I do remember coming to a dead end trying to find a current listing for what I recall was the maternal grandfather. It seems that his name vanished from our records about two years ago. That could mean that he died or that he moved out of Alberta. I don't know which.

She then recalled, "I do remember that the mother's first name was Marion, and the grandmother's name was Helen, but they did not appear in our records at all." Hearing those two names, my heart started pounding with silent excitement. We continued discussing all that the Administrator had done. I was hoping that at some point she might remember that very crucial surname and blurt it out without realizing it. However, after about one hour there didn't seem to be anything that Mrs. Adams could assist me with at the moment.

Wishing to continue our relationship, I asked her if I could bring Jennifer's Adoption Order and background information to her. I timidly suggested that perhaps something in those documents may help her remember that all-important surname. Also, I felt that Mrs. Adams had notes at work with information written on them, and perhaps if she knew I was returning to her home, she may look at those notes before our second visit.

She replied, "Yes, that would be fine."

The next day I photocopied Jennifer's adoption documents. Two days later I drove to Mrs. Adams home, parked and started to walk up to her house. I met her coming out of her front door, apparently on her way out. I greeted her politely and handed her the documents. I did not have the courage to ask her if she now remembered Jennifer's surname.

Mrs. Adams then said voluntarily, "I looked again, but there are no records for Marion's father during the past two years. I tried phoning his last known telephone number, but it has been disconnected. I looked in the telephone book in Calgary, and although there are five and a half columns of that surname, I could not see him listed.

"Thank you for trying," I added. I turned around, waved, got into my car, and drove away. Once out of site, I laughed and cheered. I was almost too excited to drive home. I now knew from what the Hospital Administrator had said and confirmed by Mrs. Adams, that the place to find Jennifer's birth name was Calgary. I knew that her mother's name was Marion, her grandmother's name was Helen, and now I knew there were five and a half columns of that surname in the Calgary Telephone Book.

The next day, I took the Calgary Telephone Book to our lunch room. I must have looked ridiculous to anyone watching me. I went through each page carefully and made a note of every name that had five and a half columns. When I was finished, I had only 8 names.

I went down to our own public library in Red Deer and looked back in that familiar 1966 Henderson's Directory and studied each of the 8 surnames. Almost completing the list, I came upon the name "Wylie." There, in what seemed like bold letters jumping out at me, was the name "Marion Wylie, medical secretary," and "Helen Wylie." Marion and Helen were listed as living at the same address. I noticed a Frank Wylie, followed by his occupation, "auto mechanic," living at a different address. This would confirm that Frank and Helen were separated as stated in the background information.

The library also had copies of the Calgary Henderson's Directories for the past few years. I could see Frank Wylie listed up until two years prior. However, since then he was not listed at all.

I made a list of Marion and Helen's neighbours back in 1966 and a list of Frank Wylie's neighbours, and telephoned all of them that evening. Unfortunately, none of them knew the whereabouts of Marion, Helen or Frank.

I questioned my husband again to find out if he knew Frank Wylie. He said that the name rang a bell, but he didn't know him personally. He also did not know a Marion or a Helen Wylie.

My husband suggested, "Why don't you phone Jerry Laydler at Southland Motors. He knows everybody who has worked in service stations and every mechanic who has worked in this city." I grabbed the telephone book and looked up the telephone number for Jerry Laydler. I dialled the number and introduced myself. I asked him, "Do you remember a service station manager from 1966 who was then 40 years old, 6 ft. tall, with blonde hair, high forehead and deep set eyes?"

There was silence at first, but then I added, "He would be about 64 years old now." There was continued silence, and then he asked, "Give me that description again!" I repeated the description.

Sandra Butler Ladwig

"That sounds like Don Campbell," he replied.

I smiled as my heart tumbled with excitement. "Thank you so very much." Then I asked, "Do you remember where he had a service station?"

"Yes, it was down by the 7-11 Store downtown."

I thanked Mr. Laidler and hung up. I went into the living room, with a bounce in my steps. "Guess who Jennifer's birth father is?" I probed my husband.

"Who?" he asked with a sparkling curiosity in his eyes.

"Don Campbell." He ran a service station where the 7-11 Store is now."

"Don Campbell!" he exclaimed. "I know Don Campbell really well. I had dinner with him and his wife in Montreal only two years ago."

"Do you know his wife?" I asked.

"Oh sure," I met her in Montreal."

I asked, "Do you remember if her name is Marion?

"No, I don't think that's her name. I think her name is something like Vivien, or Virginia, or Victoria."

I sat across from my husband watching him think. He then went to the telephone, muttering, "By golly, I think Don did get his girlfriend pregnant, but I think they had a boy. I think he married her, but it doesn't seem to me that her name was Marion. Let me phone a friend of mine."

He dialled a friend of his, and as they spoke, I eavesdropped on their conversation. Then Fred asked him if he knew where Don Campbell and his wife live now. Fred kept muttering "uh huh!" "uh huh!" over and over again. Then it sounded like his friend had passed the phone to his friend's wife.

When Fred got off the telephone, he said, "I have the whole story. Don's wife was dying of cancer about the time he started dating a girl named Marion. After about 4 years, Marion got pregnant, but Don didn't feel it right that he divorce his wife when she was dying. Marion gave birth to a little girl and apparently everybody was pressuring her to put her baby up for adoption.

Finally, since nobody was supportive of her keeping her baby, one day she made the decision to place her for adoption. Then Marion moved down east and became a model. Her agent didn't like her name, and therefore she legally changed her name to "Victoria." A few months later, Don's wife died. Evidently Don then went down east to find Marion. It took him quite a while to find her. He convinced her that he loved her, and they were married."

Fred went on to explain that two years ago, Marion was introduced to him as "Victoria."

Since the correct Don Campbell could be difficult to find in a city as big as Montreal, I asked my husband if he knew anyone who may have Don's telephone number. He told me that he had a friend in Vancouver that was very close friends with Don. My husband phoned his friend in Vancouver, and after a long conversation bringing them up to date with one another, Fred finally received Don and Victoria's address and telephone number in Montreal. I watched impatiently as Ron wrote it down.

Although it was very late in the evening, I telephoned

Jennifer anyway. I blurted out in total excitement "I know your birth mother and birth father's names." I went on to tell her that they had married one another just a few years after Jennifer's birth.

"How did you find out? Tell me everything," she asked. I told her all about the Hospital Administrator, the Supervisor of Motor Vehicles and all about Jerry Laydler. I told her all about my husband's telephone calls.

Jennifer said, "I am going to phone my birth mother first thing in the morning. I will phone you right after. She was so excited that I thought she would not be able to sleep that night. I suggested it might be a great idea for her to sit down with pen and paper and write down everything she was feeling that very evening. In years to come she may appreciate reading those notes.

The next day I waited and waited. Finally Jennifer telephoned me in mid-afternoon. She told me that she had tried to phone Victoria early in the morning, but there was no answer. She tried every hour and then at noon a lady answered. Jennifer said that she introduced herself as Jennifer Wylie, phoning from Alberta. She went on to explain to Victoria that she was born in 1966 and had been placed for adoption shortly after her birth. She added that she thought it had been a very difficult decision for her mother to make.

Jennifer continued her conversation with Victoria, saying that since Victoria's maiden name had been Wylie, perhaps she may be related to Jennifer's birth mother Marion Wylie. Asking if Victoria could make some discreet inquiries for her, Victoria said, "This is a very cruel and painful joke because my baby died many years ago." That response frightened Jennifer. Even as Victoria demanded to know who she was, Jennifer could hardly continue speaking. Finally Jennifer gave Victoria her birth date, place of birth and all of the information that the government had provided to her about her birth mother and her birth father.

Jennifer said that there was silence on the telephone, and then Victoria said, "Can this be true? Could you really be my little baby Jennifer?" During a two hour conversation, Victoria said that after she had placed Jennifer for adoption, she could not live with what she had done. At some point she said that she went over the edge.

Victoria explained that after she and Don had married, they went back to Family & Social Services asking if perhaps their baby was in an orphanage or in a foster home. They both went back to that office several times during the next few weeks they were in Alberta. They hoped somebody at the counter would give them some sort of information about their little baby Jennifer they could believe and rely on. Finally, on the last visit, a Social Worker told Victoria and Don, "I am sorry to tell you this, but your baby died."

In the weeks, months and years to come, after periodic traumas and psychiatric treatments, Victoria was convinced their baby girl was dead. She said she tried not to blame Don.

Not long after that, Victoria had become pregnant. When their baby girl was born, both she and Don agreed to name her "Jennifer" after their little baby that had died. During the next four years, they had two sons.

Victoria ended their conversation by saying she was going to phone Don at work. Jennifer was pleased for the moment to have time to absorb all that Victoria had told her that afternoon.

As told to me later, Victoria telephoned Don at work. She said to him, "You better sit down, because when I tell you who just phoned me, you may fall down." He had replied, "Okay, I'm sitting." Then Victoria said, "Our daughter Jennifer just phoned me." Don interrupted, "And what did she want?" Then Victoria said, "No! Our first daughter Jennifer!" Don gasped in disbelief and then dashed right home. When their children came home from school that afternoon, Victoria sat them down and told them the secret she had been keeping from them all of these years. They had not known they had a little baby sister who had died. That evening the Campbell family telephoned Jennifer, and a new and wonderful relationship began.

Two days later, Jennifer flew to Montreal and spent a week with her birth family. During that week I received a telephone call from Don and Victoria, thanking me for my perseverance in finding them.

I had occasion to meet Jennifer in Edmonton. She and I spent an afternoon with her grandfather, Frank Wylie who was now living in a nursing home in Edmonton. His only phone number was the main switchboard of the Home. He no longer drove a car..

Three months later, while my husband and I were in Montreal at an automotive convention. I walked up to Don. He looked at my name tag and proclaimed, "Oh! – Family!"

We had dinner with Don and Victoria that evening. I was delighted to meet both of them, Victoria, with her fair complexion, green eyes and blonde hair, and Don with his deep set blue eyes, high forehead, grey hair and jovial personality. The two of them seemed like teenagers who had just fallen in love. After dessert, Victoria leaned over to me and whispered. "I had a secret for many years that I have never told anyone. I blamed myself for Jennifer's death. I prayed I would die so that I could be with my little baby in Heaven, but now, I feel like I am in Heaven, with our whole family together at last."

This is the true story of Victoria's secret.

CHAPTER THIRTEEN

THE WOLF RAVEN

When an adoptee has been searching for a birth mother for years and years, it is because of his unsuccessful attempts and absolute frustration that he becomes extremely sensitive to the slightest hint he may receive from a social worker in the province where he was born.

Steve was born and relinquished for adoption in Alberta. His birth name was "Robert Schmidt." He found it almost impossible to find his birth mother in Alberta by searching for her from his home in Parksville, B.C. Therefore, he and his wife Mary decided to devote their vacation to travelling to Alberta to find Steve's birth mother.

Steve and Mary travelled to Edmonton, Alberta. They made an appointment with a Social Worker to discuss the information in his adoption file. Steve sat across from a social worker who had his file opened in front of her. Unfortunately she tilted the file toward herself so Steve could not read anything upside down. The social worker told him his birth mother was a waitress with a grade 10 education, belonged to the United Church and was of Ukrainian nationality.

Seeing the pain and frustration on Steve's face, the social worker evidently tried to help him by providing him with a scenario. She said, "Say for example – that your birth mother's name was Ann," ...... She then went on to provide Steve with tips on how to find his birth mother. Leaving Edmonton that year, Steve was ecstatic that he now knew his birth mother's name was "Ann Schmidt." Steve spent two years trying to find Ann Schmidt.

In late October of 1989, Steve and Mary travelled back to Alberta to find Ann Schmidt. My telephone rang one evening. Steve and Mary were in Calgary and asked me if they could come to visit me in Red Deer the next evening to gain my assistance in a search for his birth mother. I agreed.

That evening Steve and his wife Mary arrived. Steve was in his late 40's, handsome, tall, slim, and had dark brown eyes and hair. Mary was medium height, very attractive, round face, grey hair, and had a warm friendly smile.

When we were comfortable at my kitchen table and had shared tidbits of information about one another, Steve brought out his Adoption Order and what is called, "Background Information." His Background Information stated that he was born on May 4, 1943, his birth mother had been a domestic, she was 19 years of age, and was from a family of three brothers and two sisters. His birth mother's parents were both living at the time of Steve's birth, and his grandfather was a farmer. That information was fairly straight forward. However, when I looked at his Adoption Order and saw his name, "Robert Schmidt," I shook my head and sighed. The surname "Schmidt" was almost as common as Smith and Jones. There were pages and pages of the name "Schmidt" in every telephone book.

Steve told me about his visit to a social worker two years ago when she had told him his birth mother's first name was "Ann." I felt that, although social workers are often sympathetic, they are not that sympathetic!

I could not believe his social worker had actually given Steve his birth mother's real Christian name. There was a Director at Social Services I was sort of acquainted with, that did say to me, "Her name starts with a C and sometimes a K." I toyed with him one time after I had found a birth mother, saying, "I suppose you are going to tell me her name is something like 'Astrid'. His reply was, "So you found her!"

I asked Steve to repeat to me the social worker's entire and exact conversation as he remembered it. He repeated the words the social worker had said to him "..... Say for example that your birth mother's name was Ann."

I was still not convinced her name was Ann, but having a name – any name, seemed to pacify Steve for the time being. Steve and Mary said they were going to go back to Edmonton the next morning and meet with the social worker. They asked for my thoughts on what they should do.

I had an idea! I took out a map of Alberta and photocopied it so it would be black and white. I then sectioned off the map in one inch squares, colouring each square in a different colour. Each square was approximately a 30 mile radius. When the map was completely sectioned off and coloured in a radius of 200 miles around Edmonton, I told Steve to take the map to the social worker he had talked to two years ago, and ask if she would give him a colour. If she was as helpful and as sensitive as Steve had portrayed her to be, perhaps she would help by giving him a further hint. To look for a Schmidt family in a 30 mile radius would be much easier than searching all over the province. Then I showed him how to search through Henderson's Directories and what each of the symbols meant.

Steve and Mary were sleeping in the back of their van. I insisted they stay inside my house where they would be warm. We all worked together cooking dinner. The next morning at 7:00 a.m. I gave them breakfast and bid them farewell. The next evening Steve telephoned me. He said:

> I showed the social worker the map, but after glancing at it, she said she could not help me because the coloured sections were not far enough north to include the town in question. However, the social worker did say that in 1943, my birth mother lived in a town that reflected itself.

> I telephoned the Town Office in North Star in the northern part of Alberta, and asked the lady who answered the phone if she could remember a Schmidt family who had lived at North Star in the 1940s. Steve explained that the father was a farmer, and they had three boys and three girls. That lady said that particular Schmidt family moved to Camrose Alberta in the 1950s. She said one of the boys was named "Marvin."

The next day Steve and Mary drove to Camrose. They went to the library in Camrose and searched through old and new telephone books and old newspapers trying to find any reference to an Ann Schmidt. The oldest Henderson's Directory for Camrose was in the year 1975. Steve said there was no reference anywhere to an "Ann Schmidt."

Steve telephoned a Marvin Schmidt listed in the phone book in Camrose, asking if he knew of a Schmidt family who had moved to Camrose from North Star Alberta. Marvin Schmidt evidently claimed he had lived at North Star, but when Steve asked him if he knew Ann Schmidt, he said he did not know anyone by that name.

Steve and Mary spent three days going through numerous newspapers on microfilm looking for the name Ann Schmidt. They took turns spinning the reels as long as their eyes would hold out. On the evening of the third day Steve telephoned me. He sounded tired, frustrated and disappointed.

"Can we come back to Red Deer?" he pleaded. "Please?"

"Of course, I replied, come on back and we'll find her from here."

The next evening when I arrived home from work, Steve and Mary were sitting in their van in my driveway. "Come on in!" I said.

Both Mary and Steve looked so cold and old and tired and hungry. Steve looked as though he had lost all hope. They told me they had been sleeping in their cold van and eating in restaurants. I had them bring in their suitcases and showed them to a bedroom. Each of them had a shower and looked so much better afterwards. When they asked if they could take my three children and me out for supper, I replied "No thanks, we are going to have a good home-cooked meal right here." When they argued, I gave them each jobs to do that helped to appease their offer to go out for dinner. We even made a big lemon pie. After dinner and dishes, we sat down at the kitchen table to talk over everything they had done in the past three days. When Steve finished telling me everything, I asked for Marvin Schmidt's phone number. I was more positive than ever that the social worker in Edmonton had only used the name "Ann" as an example.

I went up to my bedroom and telephoned Marvin Schmidt in Camrose. On the pretence of going to school with his sisters, I asked him where his sisters are now. He sounded delighted to bring me up to date on his family's whereabouts and who each of them had married. He gave me his sisters' phone numbers. He was very friendly and found pleasure in talking about North Star. I inquired briefly as to which of his sisters had been born about 1924. "Oh, that would be my sister Betty. Her name is now Betty Coleman and she lives in Lethbridge. He gave me her phone number.

As I walked down to my kitchen, Steve and Mary stopped talking and looked at me. I sat down and explained that I had telephoned Marvin Schmidt and that he gave me the married name and phone number of one of his sisters who may have known Ann Schmidt. I faked it because I now knew Steve's birth mother's name was really "Betty".

I suggested Steve telephone her. "Tell her your name

and ask her for her assistance. Tell her your birth name was Robert Schmidt and that you were born in Edmonton on May 4, 1943. Tell her you were adopted by wonderful parents. However, you have always had a desire to find your birth mother and become friends with her. If she asks why you are phoning her, tell her that since her maiden name was Schmidt, you are hoping that someone in her family may have known your birth mother, such as a sister, an aunt or a cousin. I then added, "Please don't give her the name Ann," and we'll see what she has to say. Tell Betty that if she should happen to find out your birth mother is a member of her family or someone she knows, would she please tell your mother on your behalf that you would dearly love to correspond with her, exchange photographs, and perhaps some day meet one another in person. Tell her that you think about your birth mother almost every day.

I also told him to ask if he can telephone her back in a week or two, or ask if she wishes to telephone him back. Give her your phone number. Also give her my phone number if she wishes to phone you back tonight or tomorrow. Then ask her to repeat the two phone numbers back to you to make sure she wrote them down correctly."

Steve looked disappointed that he may have to wait a week or two, but he agreed to make the phone call to Betty Coleman. I took him up to my bedroom, sat him by my phone, gave him paper and a pen and shut the door behind me. On my way back to the kitchen I crossed my fingers.

Mary and I sat at the kitchen table talking for about

twenty minutes. Then we both looked at the phone in the kitchen, wondering. We continued our discussions about how many years Steve had been searching for his birth mother.

Mary told me how Steve had been so hopeful years before and how frustrated he has been in not finding Anne. "It had always seemed to be so important to him to have biological roots. He has also wondered if he has any brothers and sisters."

Then we talked about Steve and Mary's three children and their lives on the Island. At this point both Mary and I again stared at the phone. "It's been 30 minutes. I wonder if he is talking to her now?" I didn't dare lift the receiver to find out.

I told Mary all about my family, the places I had lived, and again 15 more minutes elapsed. We again stared at the phone. Mary and I were about to begin a second pot of coffee when I had an idea. I crept up to the bedroom and listened at the door. There was not a sound from inside the bedroom. I crept back. I shook my head at Mary. We both laughed at ourselves because of the mystery and intrigue we were creating.

We started talking about Steve again. Then 10 minutes later, we heard the bedroom door open. We stopped in the middle of our conversation. We heard every footstep as Steve came down the four steps. Mary and I both glanced at Steve for some kind of a sign on his face. Then he approached us. He put out his left arm and curled it around my neck. Then he put out his right arm and curled it around Mary's neck. He pulled each of us into his face as though in a hug. He smiled, shut his eyes, and his entire body shook as he said, "It was her! It was her!"

Mary and I began to laugh and clap, shout out loud and then stand up and jump up and down as we Western Canadians often do. Steve was laughing and crying at the same time.

We were so loud my three children came running into the kitchen to see what was happening. When I told my children what was happening, they smiled and stood quietly at the table to listen as well.

"What did she say Steve," I asked, "What did she say?"

"I have it right here on tape," he said. He took a small tape machine out of his pocket and set it down on the kitchen table. He rewound the tape and pushed "play." We all listened intently:

"Ring.

"Hello.

"Hello – Could I speak with Betty Coleman please?"

"Yes, speaking."

"My name is Steve Johnson. I am visiting here in your lovely province, and while I am here I am trying to find some relatives of mine by the name of Schmidt. I understand that your maiden name was Schmidt."

"Yes, it was."

"My request is a little out of the ordinary. You see, I was adopted."

(There was a long pause)

"Uh hum."

"I was born on May 4, 1943 and my mother named me Robert Schmidt. Shortly after my birth, my mother found that she just could not raise me alone, so out of her love for me in wanting me to have both a mother and a father and a good and loving home, she decided to place me for adoption."

"I see.

"I was adopted by wonderful people and have had a good life, but I have always wanted to find my birth mother. I have searched for her for many years.

"I am wondering Mrs. Coleman, if you could possibly make some very discreet inquiries in your family to see if my birth mother could be one of your relatives, such as a sister, a cousin or maybe an aunt? I don't know very much about her other than the fact that she was 19 years old when I was born. She was from a family of three brothers and two sisters, and her father was a farmer."

"Well, I don't know."

"I would be very grateful to you if you could please assist me. I so much want to find my mother.

"Well, I guess I could try."

"If you happen to find out who my birth mother is, could you please tell her that I think of her every year on my birthday. I would like to write letters to her and exchange photographs and perhaps some day she and I could meet in person.

"I would want her to know that I will never interfere in her life if there is some reason she doesn't want to see me."

"Well, I doubt she would feel that way."

"I am so hopeful that you can possibly find her for me. The only Christian name I have for her is Ann.

(There was a long pause)

Sandra Butler Ladwig

"Her name isn't Ann. I am the one you are trying to find."

"What, you mean – really – you are my mother?"

"Yes, I am your mother if you are who you say you are."

"I can hardly believe this. All this time I have been trying to find an Ann Schmidt and your name is really Betty?"

"Your name is Steve did you say?"

"Yes."

"Well Steve, I am your Mother. I have so much to say to you. This is my wish come true. Where are you?"

It was about this point that the darned tape ran out, but Steve said that they made arrangements to meet at a shopping mall in Lethbridge. She evidently said to him, "I don't want you to get lost trying to find my house. I lost you once, I'm not going to lose you again."

In the morning Steve and Mary left for Lethbridge. Several days later, prior to Steve and Mary leaving the province, Steve telephoned me to say they had had a wonderful visit with Betty and they were all very happy. He said Betty telephoned her daughter, Steve's sister, and told her to put the coffee on. "I am bringing somebody over to meet you." Steve said when they walked up the front steps of his sister's home he wondered what Betty would say to her daughter.

When Betty's daughter opened her front door Betty simply explained, "Before I met your father I had a baby and put him up for adoption. This is him. His name is Steve."

Steve said his sister stared at her mother and then

stared at him. She then threw her arms around him and kissed him. They all spent the entire afternoon together.

Steve wrote a letter to me a month later, telling me his sister and her family from Lethbridge came to Parksville to visit with them. On the way up the Island two other brothers and their families also came to Parksville to meet Steve and Mary. Steve said, "We had a wonderful weekend together." Steve enclosed a photograph of himself and his extended family. Looking at the men in the picture, I couldn't tell which one was actually Steve because they all looked so much alike.

Along with Steve's letter and pictures, he sent a gift. It was a beautiful but strange looking animal carved by one of the West Coast Indians.

The West Coast Indians are said to carve from a very practical point of view, keenly observing the natural world, especially the animals in that world. The artists exaggerate the eyes, nose and ears of a wolf to signify the keen senses of the wolf. Likewise, the teeth signified the wolf's strong jaw. Also, by working a Raven theme into the legs, and feathers into the body, the artist has pointed out a wolf's remarkable ability to travel swiftly over great distances. Survival, after all, depended on hunting skills. Carved on the back are the words "The Wolf Raven."

Author's note: All of the carvings of the West Coast Indians have very deep meanings, and each and every mark made on the animals or the birds is created in the form of an Indian canoe. A Raven is a very fast bird indeed, as is a wolf, both known for their persistence. (Now that was Steve.)

It is said that when Noah was trying to find out if there was land up ahead, he sent out a Raven.

CHAPTER FOURTEEN

MARTIN LUTHER KING BOULEVARD
ROUTE 137 NORTH OF BUTLER

I am including this story because what I did may help countless others searching for a long lost loved-one in the United States.

Butler had to be an omen since that is my maiden name and also the name of my nephew Brian Butler who lived in Atlanta Georgia. Brian is an avid pool player who travels all over North America to play in numerous pool tournaments.

One fall evening while playing pool, Brian met a young pool player by the name of Larry LeMay. During the evening, they began talking about their lives. Larry told my nephew he had been born in New York, but his father moved he and his two sisters to Orlando Florida when they were small children. He explained that – when he and his sisters were in their teens, their father swiftly moved all of them to Atlanta.

Larry said after his father died, a relative of theirs told

him he and his two sisters were taken by their father to Orlando and then to Atlanta, stealing them away from their Mother who lived in New York. Hearing that, Larry said he hired a detective to find his Mother so they could be reunited with her, but after paying hundreds of dollars, the detective came up empty-handed. The problem was that neither Larry nor his sisters knew their mother's name. Larry was 27 years old at the time and his two sisters were 26 and 25.

Brian, in his wisdom, suggested he contact his Auntie Sandy, who he knew "can find anybody." A few weeks later, I received a long letter from Larry LeMay. He explained all about his father's secret, the detective he had hired and his desire to find his Mother.

The first thing I did was send three letters to Larry – one to be signed by him, one to be signed by his sister Patricia and one to be signed by his sister Mary. All of the letters were requests for their birth certificates. The letters stated that each was enclosing a copy of their Driver's License (or photo ID), and a utility or telephone Bill addressed to each of them – all for authenticity of who they are. The letters were addressed to the New York State Department of Health, Vital Records Certification Unit, Menands, New York. I asked each of them enclose a money order for $45.00, requesting Priority Handling, which would mean each of them would receive their birth certificates in about two weeks, rather than four months. Their birth certificates would give them the name of their Mother, her maiden name, and where she was born.

When Larry received his birth certificate he immediately sent me a photocopy of it. His Mother's name was Mary Louise LeMay, maiden name Edwards. His father's name was Michael James LeMay, which Larry already knew.

Martin Luther King has and will always go down in history as the man who changed the world, "the Whole World," when he brought about rights and freedoms for all African Americans.

I sent a letter to Larry to sign and mail – addressed to the Social Security Office on Martin Luther King Boulevard in Atlanta. I explained to Larry that his Mother would have turned 66 years old a few months ago according to his birth certificate. The letter stated:

> My name is Larry LeMay. My two sisters and I were stolen from our Mother when we were very small children. Our father, Michael James LeMay, took us to Orlando Florida, thinking that our mother, Mary Louise LeMay, would never find us there.
>
> Then our father caught wind that our mother found out that we were in Florida and she evidently moved there. We were in our teens at the time. Our father then moved all of us to Atlanta, thinking that she would never find us here.
>
> We asked our father about our Mother, but he made us promise that we would never ask questions about her ever again. Our father died last year.
>
> We only recently received our birth certificates which told us that our Mother's name is Mary Louise LeMay, maiden name Edwards, who would have turned 66 years old only a few months ago. We are wondering if

you could please check your records to see if you can find out where our Mother is living and receiving her monthly Social Security benefits. If you can find out where she is, I wonder if you would please forward the enclosed letter addressed to her.

The letter that I enclosed for Larry to sign and include read:

Our Very Dear Mother: We have just recently found out your name and have asked the Social Security Office to send you this letter.

My sisters and I were taken to Orlando Florida when we were very young. In our teens, we were taken to Atlanta. Our father died about a year ago.

We were told by one of our father's relatives that our father stole us from you. You must have been frantic not knowing where we were. I hired a Detective to find you, but he was unsuccessful.

My friend, who is helping us, telephoned the New York Police Department, Missing Persons Bureau, thinking that you may have filed a Missing Persons Report, but they told her they have thousands of missing person reports but they have no records dating back to when we left New York.

My sisters and I would be so thrilled if this letter reaches you. If you receive this letter, please telephone me immediately at 1-404-973-5080. You can phone me collect for sure.

I am mailing this letter today and will be waiting by the telephone in the evenings for the next few weeks. Please do not be afraid to telephone me. Whatever happened in the past – is in the past. Martin Luther King says – 'Hate cannot drive out hate; only love can do that.'

We need your love and we are hoping that you need our love too.

Your son, Larry LeMay"

Like so many searches I have done in the past, I did not expect to hear from Larry after his search was a success, as I knew it would be. Martin Luther King Boulevard was the magical address. I did receive a letter from Larry. It read:

> I received a letter from a lady at the Social Security Office. She said that this was her last day working there, but she could not leave her desk without searching for our Mother. She said she did find our Mother living in Orlando Florida and she sent my letter on to her. She wished us good luck.

Larry went on to say

> About a week after I received the letter from the Social Security Office, I received a phone call from our Mother.

> She was crying on the telephone, saying how happy she was to finally find us. She gave me her telephone number and her address. I drove down to Orlando to meet with her in person and to hug her. She is now moving to Atlanta in order to finally be reunited with my two sisters and I.

> I cannot thank you enough Sandra for giving us back our Mother. We would never have found her without your help.

I wrote this story in order to explain to those searching for someone in the adoption triangle – that the Social Security Offices in the U.S. can and will assist, as long as your explanation is valid and of course heart-warming as this one is.

I would love to send this story to Oprah and to Barack Obama.

CHAPTER FIFTEEN

ONE WAY TO CONTACT A BIRTH MOTHER

This is definitely not a "how to" direction – it is only a suggestion. There are many ways to contact a birth mother, however, I can tell you that saying, "Does March 4, 1951 mean anything to you?" is definitely never a good thing to ask. Also, I would suggest all adoptees never contact an Aunt, Uncle or a Cousin and tell them the truth of why you are calling. A birth mother may not have told anyone in her family about giving birth to her baby and placing her baby for adoption, and therefore it is wrong for you to tell them now. Also, please please do not ever have a husband, a wife or a child make this all-important call on your behalf, unless the adoptee is incapacitated. It is like stealing one of the most important moments in an adoptee's life. I learned this, but only after I had contacted a very few birth mothers.

The scenario here is that – after a birth mother has been found, the following could be the dialogue:

Dial her number. "Hello."

"May I please speak to Sandra Myers?"

"Speaking."

"I would like to talk to you about a very pleasant, personal matter. I could phone you back later if you are not alone."

"No, go ahead – I am alone."

"I was born on March 4, 1951. Shortly after my birth I was placed for adoption. I am sure it was a very difficult decision for my Mother to make."

"My surname was "Myers.""

"I understand your maiden name was Myers. I am wondering if you could possibly make some very discreet inquiries in your family to see if you can find out who my birth mother is.

"If you do happen to find out who she is, I would want her to know that it is not my intention to infringe upon her or her family in any way. I just would love to meet her if she would like to meet me.

"I don't know much about my birth mother. She was 18 years old when I was born. She worked as a secretary. She put down on her documents that she was 5'-10" with auburn hair and brown eyes.

"My documents state she had absolutely no support from her family or my birth father. She said she wanted me to have a good home and be raised by a mother and a father."

I want to stop here for a moment of explanations. If Sandra says she has company, ask her when you can phone her back. If she insists on knowing why you are calling, just simply say that it is a very pleasant personal matter and that you will fully explain when you phone her back. She may already have an inkling of why you are calling. She may be anxious to talk to you and therefore ask that you phone her back in an hour.

If she asks how you know her name is "Myers," just say you had a researcher helping you and therefore you don't know.

When you are giving her information about your birth mother, for Heaven sakes don't tell her all that you know about her. She may feel threatened at how much you know.

Then carry on your conversation as follows.

"If you do happen to find out who my Mother is, would you please tell her this:

"I want her to know that I have had a good life, and I have great parents.

"Please tell her I would love to meet her. If she lives far away, perhaps we can correspond or talk on the phone. Then some day I want to meet my Mother – face to face and give her a big hug.

"If my Mother has not told her husband or her children about me, she does not have to tell them now. She and I can meet in private whenever and wherever she chooses.

"Do you think you can help me?"

At this point she may say "yes."

What we have done here is to tell her all about why you are phoning her without backing her into a corner.

Then say, "Could I please give you my telephone number, and can you make inquiries within your family and then phone me back in a week or so?" She will likely say "yes" because she will want to think about this. She may want to tell her husband and children before she phones you back. Make absolutely sure that she repeats your phone number. A birth mother is quite nervous or excited and may take down your phone number wrong, perhaps reversing two numbers.

Then say "Goodbye."

At this point I would suggest you do your laundry, vacuum, dust, wash the walls, wash the floors, wash the kids and wash the dog. Do not go outside. Try to stay home. Most birth mothers will phone back the next day.

Your birth mother might, at any point, say, "I am your Mother!" Then you can just simply chat with one another.

I had one adoptee, (a radio announcer in Toronto) that said he had decided what he was going to say. When his birth mother said "hello," all he could remember was what I told him to say. It worked out perfectly.

If you are going to be nervous, write out what you want to say but try not to sound like you are reading it.

Good luck.

(Thousands of birth mothers, birth fathers, siblings, and adoptive parents are standing with you touching your shoulders. You are never alone. Remember, when you are making telephone calls and not being truthful, people are not stupid, but they are understanding. One man who held the hospital records of a small hospital on the Island gave Roxanne the name of the woman who gave birth to a baby on that day and then he added a P.S. "I can't help but wonder if you are that little baby.")

BIRTH MOTHER CONTACTING AN ADOPTEE

Several birth mothers do not want to infringe upon the lives of the child they placed for adoption. She, or they, may choose to just rely on the Post Adoption Registry or wait until their child comes looking for them. If a birth mother wishes to make contact, the adoptee may answer her by saying, "I have been searching for you for many years but always came up against a brick wall. I am so glad that you found me......" Or, an adoptee may say, "I wanted to search for you, but didn't know how to go about it. I am so glad that you found me."

I spoke with a friend of mine who is a birth mother. I asked her about a birth mother contacting her child, and she said one way to do it is to send a "Double Registered" letter to her adult child. Say in the letter that you will phone her on Thursday at 10:00 a.m. If she does not answer the phone on Thursday at 10:00 a.m., then try again a week later and two weeks later. (He/she may be in Arizona for the winter. If she is away for the winter months, perhaps her mail will be forwarded to her by someone picking up her mail.) A double registered letter must be signed for and therefore, after a lengthy period of time the card and letter will be returned to you not signed for. You may then know that she is not at home. You can then send the letter again – this time by regular mail.

If none of these ideas should work, then phone your adult child. If you have an address, you can go and see if there are any cars in the driveway. If it appears that nobody is home, then go to a neighbour or both neighbours. Make up a believable story and then ask the neighbours if they know where Sandra is. Then you will know why nobody signed for your letter. It can be a long and tedious plan, but it is worth while in the end. This method is tedious, however, you have to know if Sandra received your letter or not.

I can tell everybody in the adoption triangle that the longer you search for a loved one, the more you will love them when found. Kahlil Gibran said the deeper your sorrow – will be the same distance as the height of your happiness. The exact quote is:

"The deeper that sorrow carves into your being, the more joy you can contain. When you are joyous, look deep into your heart and you will find that it is only that which has given you sorrow that is now giving you joy."

In over 500 searches that I did personally, I have never known of a birth mother not wanting to know about her child and most want to have a relationship with their child. There have only been one or two out of 500 that did not want to have a relationship with the child they relinquished for adoption. I have never known of an adoptee not wanting to be contacted by her birth mother. Same goes for all of the birth fathers and all of the siblings out there. Which one of us would not love to find out that there is one more of us out there some-where? The true story "Switched at Birth" is unusual, as is the stupidity of the social worker who sent one Asian twin to the U.S. and the other to south-east Asia. My only conclusion is that we are all related anyway, one way or another.

Sandra Butler Ladwig

CHAPTER SIXTEEN

WHERE TO FIND INFORMATION

1. You can phone the Alberta Government Rite Number from anywhere in Alberta at 310-0000 and you will be passed on to the Alberta Post Adoption Registry at 780-427-6387 free of charge. If you live outside of Alberta, the number is 1-780-417-2711 but you may have to pay long distance charges.

2. On your computer type in "Alberta Post Adoption Registry forms." Then under that, click on "Request for Forms of Adoption Information."

3. When you request the background information on your birth mother and birth father or request information about your relinquished child, you will have to provide the Registry with two pieces of Identification so they will know that you are who you say you are.

4. Along with requesting your Adoption Order and background information on your birth parents you can also fill out the Post Adoption Registry form. Once they receive your registration information, they will register you in their Post Adoption Registry. After you are registered, they will carry out a search of their Registry to see if anybody is registered looking for

you. Some BM's that do not want to infringe on their child's adopted life will at least register. When you fill out the form be sure to check off BM, BF **and** siblings. Adoptees should make sure that they include "siblings."

5. Prior to 2005 a BM or BF could file a VETO. If a BM filed a Veto, this will not cover the BF and vice-versa. Almost all who filed a Veto cancelled it later on. An adoptive parent cannot file a Veto unless it is a matter of life and death.

6. On your computer go to "Alberta Post Adoption Registry." On that website you will see their address, phone number and a listing of all of their services, all kinds of tips and information and their forms.

7. Henderson's Directories are available at the Edmonton Public Library, the Calgary Public Library, the Provincial Archives, and I gifted over 900 Henderson's Directories for Edmonton, Calgary, all small and big cities in Alberta, B.C., Saskatchewan and large cities in B.C., Manitoba and Ontario – to the Glenbow Museum in Calgary. (We will talk about the Glenbow later.)

   a. Let's use the name "Sandra Ann Myers" as an example of the birth name of our adoptee. Now, if you were born in 1953 in Edmonton (Calgary same), go to the Edmonton Public Library and take the books, three at a time over to the photocopier, i.e. 1950, 1951 and 1952. (We will want to photocopy three at a time all the way up to 1975 and then skip to 1980, 1985, 1990 and 1995. Open 1950 (three years before) and photocopy the surname "Myers" and do the same for each year as I have suggested. Make absolutely sure the **year** is noted on the photocopy; otherwise write it on your photocopy. Some directories do not state the year – so make sure to write the year on top of each photocopy. (Do not even think of writing the names on a scribbler. You will be sorry you did because those photocopies will be the major part of your research material.)

b.   Now, after you have photocopied all of the names, go for Lunch. When you are having lunch, look at the years 1952-53-54 and see if you can see your mother's occupation as noted in the background information the Alberta Registry gave you. Let's give the example, "Nurse." If you do not have your mother's first name, then look for a nurse. Write those names down in your scribbler.

c.   Also, be sure to write down her address. See if she is listed with an "r" (resident) beside her name or an "h" (head of the house) beside her name. Now, after you have had lunch and a rest from the library, go back.

d.   Okay – let's say you either have her Christian name(s) or you see her name as a nurse – i.e. "Sandra Ann Myers." Go to that very year in the Henderson's Directory when you saw her listed. We are now interested in the address where she lived, i.e. 8075-80 Ave. Go to the back of the Henderson's Directory (say 1953) to the address section. Go to 80th Avenue and then to 8075 and see who owned that house. Let's say she was listed as "r" (a resident) – then we will want to see who was the (h) head of the house where she lived. That name could be her brother, her married sister or a friend.

e. Mr. Don Butler owned that house. While you are on that address page, make a list of the neighbours in your scribbler or photocopy that page (you will be glad you did. We may want to phone one or two neighbours to see if they know where Sandra is now.) Go to the front of that book and look under "Butler, Don, pipefitter, (Gwen), 8075-80 Ave. See also if Gwen is listed separately as it will give her occupation. Maybe Don Butler and/or Gwen Butler are still alive in the newest Henderson's Directory or the telephone book for Edmonton (Calgary). You can repeat all of this for years where Sandra is still listed. When she disappears – that is possibly the year she got married. (I seem to remember that there were no Henderson's Directories published after 1995.

8. If you are unable to go to the main libraries in Edmonton or Calgary, you can go to your local library and you can order pages from their Henderson's Directories to be sent to you (inter-library-loan). There is a form to fill out. Make sure your request is specific. You have to have a library card in order to do this. After you receive and study the sheets, you can send for more information as noted above. It is tedious to do it this way. You can either go to the library yourself and get the information you require in one day, or you can go the way of "Interlibrary Loan"

and take two months to receive the information you need. You will have to pay for all of the photocopies, which could be a total of about $5.00. Check off on the form that you are willing to pay.

a. You can also send for History Books from any town in Alberta that has one. It will be loaned to you by your library once it is received.

b. You can order reels of newspapers to be sent to your library, say for example – to look up an Obituary or a birth announcement.

9. When you have all of the information you require, take your gems home (otherwise you may go blind). Put a yellow mark on top of any names that are vital, i.e. BM's name, her parents, any brothers listed at the same address, etc. When you see your birth mother has a brother or sister and it notes their ages on your background information, figure out what those years would be when they were 16 years old and onward. Make photocopies of those years that they are listed. Put each page into a plastic 3-ring protector sheet, one front/one back.

a. While you are at it, obtain a 3-ring binder, possibly 3". Put all of your adoption documents, Henderson's Directory sheets, pages from your scribbler, your thoughts from time to time (you will love that years from now) and a carbon copy of every letter you write. Also, make a note of all of the telephone calls you have made and what the discussions were.

b. If you want to make notes, keep those notes in ONE scribbler. Do not have little notes here and there because you will lose them. Also, you will want to keep those notes in order. Put a date on everything. You would be surprised at how often you will refer to your notes.

10. You can go to the Provincial Archives in Edmonton at 8555 Roper Road, NW, – 86 St. and 51 Ave. (access off of Whitemud Freeway at either 91 St. or 75 St. They are **CLOSED** Sundays and Mondays. They are open Tuesday to Saturday, 9: am to 4:30 pm. They will not retrieve material between 11:30 am and 1:00 pm and not after 3:30 p.m. To be on the safe side – because the Archives is often short staffed on Saturdays, they would appreciate it if you would phone them on Friday and order the material you want to research on Saturday and they will retrieve it and put all of it on a table for you to use on Saturday.

    a. The Provincial Archives has Henderson's Directories (not for photocopying), town History Books (not for photocopying) , birth, death, marriage and divorce records. They also have "homesteader" records providing that your relative was the first homesteader.

11. The Glenbow Museum in Calgary has an abundance of records, but keep in mind that all records for the entire province are at the Provincial Archives in Edmonton. The one thing the Glenbow Museum does have is an index system right there on the research floor. Those index cards list all of the newspaper clippings about semi or prominent people. (Worth a look!)

12. The main libraries in Edmonton and Calgary have

"Voter's Polls." If you have an address, you can look up that address in the Voter's Polls and see who else was living at that address. One of those libraries has names first and then addresses and the other one has addresses and then the names. You can see who all lived at the same address as your birth mother in the years where you are looking. Those books are huge and heavy. (Use a cart.)

13. There is a Genealogical Society in each of the large cities. I believe they have regular meetings that a person can attend.

14. Latter Day Saints in Red Deer has census records. I made friends with a man at the Canada Census office and he gave me all of the Myers names in 1953. I could then compare a birth mother's birth date with her age that was provided to me in my background information. (Good luck!)

15. When I found out a grandfather's land on a farm, in a small town or in a city, I was able to go to the Land Titles Office and go back in old books containing Certificates of Title and see who that land was transferred to. You can then come forward in those books up to the present day to see who owns that land now. You cannot take a municipal address to Land Titles, but you can take a municipal address to City Hall or a town office and they will give you the legal description.

16. The Red Deer Museum and Archives has central Alberta newspapers on microfilm. They also have a listing of death records on a CD. (I am sure Edmonton and Calgary also have those CD's) The staff will help

you set it up. The deceased people are listed in alphabetical order. Across that line is a notation of where the person is buried or where the information was taken from. The location of a cemetery is helpful in looking in that town or city's phone book or sending for that town's History Book.

17. I had one occasion where I found out, after $7,000.00 and 25 years of searching, that ALL of the information on an Adoptee's background information was an out and out **lie.** The only way to overcome this problem is to send for an Ancestry DNA Kit. The Kit costs somewhere between $75.00 and $120.00. Once you receive the Kit, make sure you do not eat or drink anything, or smoke at least two hours before you spit. When you put the vial into the box provided, put a little piece of tape at both ends of the box and then mail it. It is postage free. The Kit will go to their office in Dublin Ireland where there are billions of DNA's to match from. I did my DNA and found my Mother's biological family listed. In some cases a person will only find a cousin or an aunt, but that is close enough to find a birth mother or a birth father and usually that cousin or aunt will help you narrow the playing field and help you find your BM. .

18. Now that you are totally confused, I have one more idea. Write a letter to your birth mother, or your grandfather and send it to the Old Age Pension Office in the province where you were born. Tell the Pension office that you are trying to find your Aunt, "Sandra Ann Myers" or your Great Uncle, "Donald James Butler." If your birth mother or her father is

65 years old or is going to be turning 65 years old in less than six months, ask the Pension Office if they would please forward your letter to your "Aunt Sandra or your Great Uncle Donald. The Old Age Pension Office has a record of all pensioners' birth names, married names, re-married names and so forth. Be careful how you word that letter because the Pension Officer will read your letter. Therefore, it has to be believable. When your Aunt Sandra (BM) receives the letter, she will know exactly who you are. When your Great Uncle (Grandfather) receives your letter, mention "Sandra" in your letter to him and he will hopefully give the letter to Sandra, and she will know who you are. (I know this is devious, but it has worked.)

19. Parent Finder groups across Canada can be found on the Internet by typing in "Parent Finders Across Canada" and then click on the province you are interested in. Alberta has the "Birth Parents/Relatives Group" located at 2147-141 Ave., Edmonton, Alberta, T5Y 1C4, Phone 1-780-473-1912. The Parent Finders National Office is now in Ottawa. They have thousands upon thousands of adoptees and birth parents listed.

Many birth mothers have said, "I have been hoping and praying for this day to come ever since the day you turned 18 years of age."

We need to make two amendments to the Alberta Child, Youth & Family Enhancement Act, keeping in mind that at the present time – **only** the parties to the Adoption Triangle can receive information about one another, i.e.

birth mother, birth father, adoptee. Wordsmithing is very important in order to make amendments so that siblings and grandparents can receive the relinquished child's information if the birth mother or birth father is deceased or incapacitated. Contacting your M.L.A. is a good place to start. If birth mother Julie is deceased, her children will be able to find their brother/sister. If Frank is deceased, his parents will be able to find their grandson/granddaughter.

The adoption records were opened here in Alberta on January 1, 2005. We knew the new Act would assist thousands of people right away, but we felt that any minor changes could be done at a later date. **That later date has now come and gone for twelve years.** The amendments could be worded as follows:

Birth Parents:
"When one or both birth parents are deceased or incapacitated, adult siblings and grandparents will be allowed to receive the information from the Post Adoption Registry that a birth mother or a birth father would have received if they were still alive or if they were not incapacitated.

Adoptee:
"When an adoptee is deceased or not capable of sending for identifying information from his/her adoption file, the adoptee's siblings, adoptive parents or grandparents will be allowed to receive all identifying information from the adoption file.

Information from other provinces can be found at

"Canada Post Adoption Registries." This site will list who to contact in government offices in each of the Canadian provinces.

Parent Finders originated in Vancouver in 1976 by Joan Vanstone, who gathered and held the "National Registry" for decades. When Joan retired, the Parent Finders National Registry was transferred to Ottawa in 2010.

One of the girls that worked alongside of Joan Vanstone in Vancouver for 30 years had the birth name "Grace Jones." Grace was born in Edmonton Alberta, but since her surname was "Jones" she felt she would never find her birth mother, but she nevertheless dedicated her time to helping other adoptees find their birth families.

Hearing this story, I took it upon myself (in secret) to phone the hospital where Grace was born. Most every success can depend on the kindness and helpfulness of the one person on the other end of the telephone. I phoned the Edmonton hospital where Grace was born, of course during the lunch hour where newcomers often covered the lunch break. I pleaded with the girl to please help me locate Grace's birth mother, after all with the name "Jones" there would never be a chance of Grace ever finding her birth mother.

The very sweet receptionist told me the sun was shining in Athabasca. I thanked her and hung up. (How many times have I felt like I just robbed a bank?)

Of course I did phone Jean (who you will remember from "Looking Over my Shoulder"). I asked her if she knew a Jones family from Athabasca. She did, and told me the birth mother in question was also named "Gwen

Jones" (which often happens). Jill told me that BM Gwen was now living in Victoria, B.C. Jean made a few inquiries and then phoned me back, giving me Gwen's married name, her address and her phone number in Victoria. I immediately relayed all of this information to Joan Vanstone in Vancouver. I imagine that was some party. I had occasion to meet Gwen and Gwen in my hotel restaurant in Victoria. Again, I couldn't help but look up.

Larry from Lacombe telephoned me one day asking if he could bring his file to me. He dropped his 2 ft. file off, (containing file folders and large school binders) at my home at 5:30 p.m. At 9:00 p.m. that evening Larry phoned me and said, "Well........ What do you think?" I asked that he give me a day or two. Diving right into his file I could see that his birth name was Michael Herman. His birth mother was a waitress in 1958. I could not see a waitress in his Henderson Directory sheets.

Now – if you could imagine a social worker sitting across a desk from a birth mother. The social worker has several forms to fill out. As she asks the birth mother questions, she fills in the empty spaces with pertinent information. When the birth mother is asked what her name is, she says, for example, my full name is Marie Elizabeth Herman. But hold on here – the social worker did not ask Marie to spell her surname. I don't know what it was in situations like this.

Did the social worker have a lunch date?
Was it near the end of the day?
Was the social worker inexperienced?
Was the social worker lacking in common sense?

Was the birth mother so frightened of social workers, nurses and society in general that she did not spell her surname, or she deliberately misspelled it – WHO KNOWS!.

I looked in my 1958 Edmonton Henderson's Directory for the name "Hermann," "Herrman" and "Herrmann". There – as bold as can be was the name "Marie Herrmann, waitress....." Digging a little deeper, I found that Marie Herrmann was from Delburne, Alberta. The history book for Delburne showed the Herrmann family – who everybody married and where they all live now..

Our friend Jean at Athabasca was born Elsie Christophersen in 1939 – birth mother Swedish. Now was that::

Christophersen (Swedish)?
Christopherson (English)?
Christoffersen, (Norwegian)? or
Christofferson (Danish)?

Jean's birth mother was said to be Swedish. The Alberta History Book on nationalities (located at most libraries) said that – during the Second World War farmers had to stay home in order to run their farms. The Swedish people farmed at Kalmar (with a "K"). I telephone the bar in Calmar and spoke with a bartender. I asked him if he knew of a Christophersen family that had lived in Kalmar during the War. He said his Aunt (now deceased) was "Elsie Christophersen." He said she died while giving birth to her baby. **(Hi Jean!)**

Names such as "Anderson" – can be spelled "Andersen." Martin can be Marten, Nelson can be

Nielson, Smith can be Schmidt, Christensen can be Christianson, Cansineau had been anglicized to Cantin, and of course MacDonald can be McDonald – and so forth. When you cannot find your birth mother using the spelling of your birth surname – try different spellings.

Since this is **your** book, you can put a yellow smear across any names or words you consider important.

I hope you will enjoy reading "The Tigers in Your Dreams" as much as I enjoyed writing it.

CHAPTER SEVENTEEN

TWO DIFFERENT KINDS OF LOVE

Once there were two women
who never knew each other.

One you do not remember –
the other you call "Mother."

Two different lives shaped
to make yours one;

One became your guiding star,
the other became your sun.

The first gave you life –
the second taught you to live it.

The first gave you a need for love,
the second was there to give it.

One gave you a nationality,
the other gave you a name.

One gave you the seeds of talent,
the other gave you an aim.

One gave you emotions,
the other calmed your fears.

One saw your first sweet smile,
the other dried your tears.

The other prayed for a child
and her hope was not denied.

And now you ask me through your tears
The age old question through the years.

"Heredity?" or "Environment?"
Which are you a product of?

Neither, my darling, neither!

Just two different kinds of love.

- Author Unknown

Sandra Butler Ladwig

To order more copies of this book, find books by other Canadian authors, or make inquiries about publishing your own book, contact PageMaster at:

PageMaster Publication Services Inc.
11340-120 Street, Edmonton, AB T5G 0W5
books@pagemaster.ca
780-425-9303

catalogue and e-commerce store
PageMasterPublishing.ca/Shop

About the Author

Sandra (Butler) Ladwig was a Parent Finder in Alberta for 49 years. She has located well over 500 missing persons and has assisted over 1000 people who just needed support and direction.

She has a twin brother George, who is a Private Investigator. George has been a great help with some of the searches Sandra has completed over the years.

Sandra worked as a legal secretary for 20 years and was able to assist the lawyers in her firm by locating the whereabouts of defendants so that they could be served with legal documents.

Sandra does, in almost all cases, teach the adoptee to make her/his own telephone call to a birth mother, birth father and siblings.

She is hoping that her true stories will not only entertain those involved in the adoption triangle, but will also provide ideas and directions for adoptees who are up against a brick wall in their own searches.